MTTC 051 Guidance Counselor
Teacher Certification Exam

By: Sharon Wynne, M.S.
Southern Connecticut State University

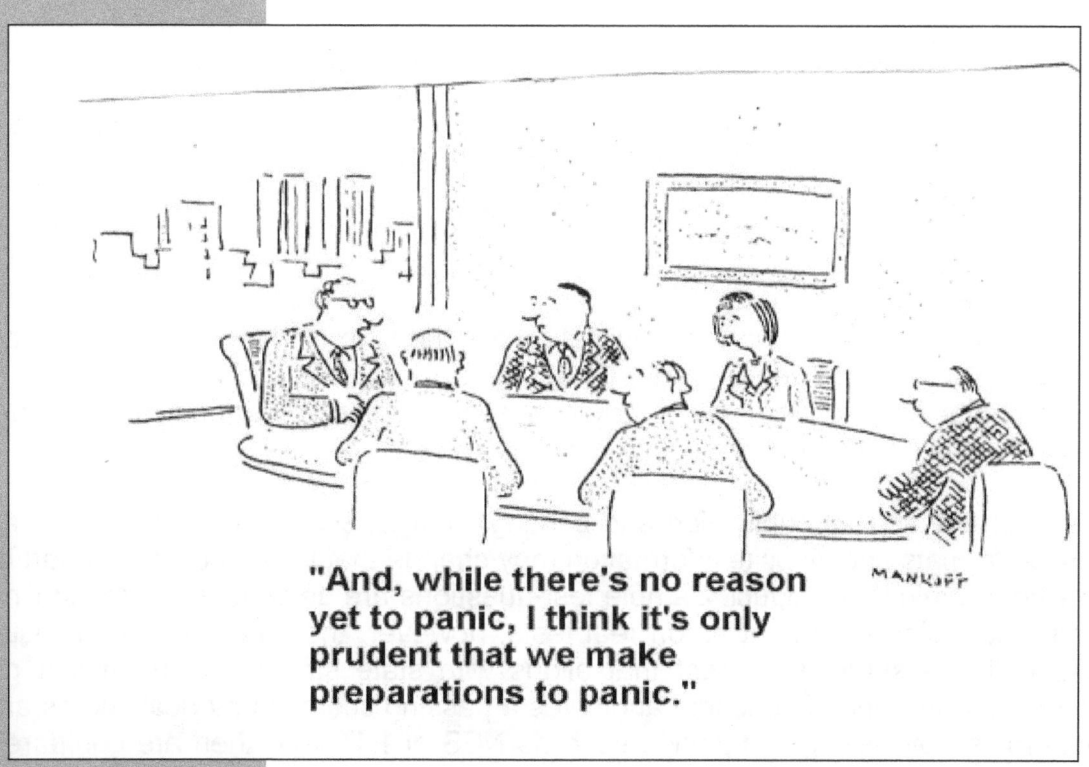

"And, while there's no reason yet to panic, I think it's only prudent that we make preparations to panic."

XAMonline, INC.
Boston

Copyright © 2008 XAMonline, Inc.
All rights reserved. No part of the material protected by this copyright notice may be reproduced or utilized in any form or by any means, electronic or mechanical, including photocopying, recording or by any information storage and retrievable system, without written permission from the copyright holder.

To obtain permission(s) to use the material from this work for any purpose including workshops or seminars, please submit a written request to:

XAMonline, Inc.
21 Orient Ave.
Melrose, MA 02176
Toll Free 1-800-509-4128
Email: info@xamonline.com
Web www.xamonline.com
Fax: 1-781-662-9268

Library of Congress Cataloging-in-Publication Data

Wynne, Sharon A.
 School Guidance & Counseling 20420: Teacher Certification / Sharon A. Wynne. -2nd ed.
 ISBN 978-1-60787-087-6
  1. School Guidance & Counseling 20420   2. Study Guides.   3. MTTC
  4. Teachers' Certification & Licensure.   5. Careers

Contributing Authors/Editors: Robin Connors   Wendy Willingham

Disclaimer:
The opinions expressed in this publication are the sole works of XAMonline and were created independently from the National Education Association, Educational Testing Service, or any State Department of Education, National Evaluation Systems or other testing affiliates.

Between the time of publication and printing, state specific standards as well as testing formats and website information may change that is not included in part or in whole within this product. Sample test questions are developed by XAMonline and reflect similar content as on real tests; however, they are not former tests. XAMonline assembles content that aligns with state standards but makes no claims nor guarantees teacher candidates a passing score. Numerical scores are determined by testing companies such as NES or ETS and then are compared with individual state standards. A passing score varies from state to state.

Printed in the United States of America

MTTC Guidance Counselor 51
ISBN: 978-1-60787-087-6

TABLE OF CONTENTS

Subarea: HUMAN DEVELOPMENT AND LEARNING

COMPETENCY 1.0 Understand human development from early childhood to adulthood 1

Skill 1.1 Major Theories of Social and Personality Development 1

Skill 1.2 Basic Milestones in Physical, Motor and Language Development 15

COMPETENCY 2.0 Understand ways in which developmental stages and external factors affect educational counseling and assessment 16

Skill 2.1 The Impact of Stress on School Performance and Students' Well-being 16

Skill 2.2 Developmental Variations 17

COMPETENCY 3.0 Understand characteristics of students with special educational needs 19

Skill 3.1 Specific Populations 19

Skill 3.2 Characteristics of Students with Cognitive Impairment 21

COMPETENCY 4.0 Understand principles of learning and motivation 23

Skill 4.1 Major Theories of Learning and Cognitive Development 23

Skill 4.2 Learning Styles and Individual Differences 25

COMPETENCY 5.0 Understand principles and methods for promoting cognitive development 29

Skill 5.1 Basic Concepts to Promote Cognitive Development 29

Skill 5.2 Study Skills 29

TEACHER CERTIFICATION STUDY GUIDE

COMPETENCY 6.0 Understand principles and methods for promoting social and personal development 31

Skill 6.1 Creating Positive School Environments 31

Skill 6.2 Effective Communication Skills 32

Skill 6.3 Interpersonal and Life Skills for Students 35

Subarea: ASSESSMENT AND EVALUATION

COMPETENCY 7.0 Understand principles and characteristics of quantitative educational measurement, evaluation, and assessment methods 37

Skill 7.1 Major Tools and Functions of Appraisal 37

Skill 7.2 Knowledge of Measurement Concepts 40

COMPETENCY 8.0 Understand how to manage, administer, and interpret a variety of educational assessment programs and instruments 42

Skill 8.1 Procedures Involved in Appraisal Administration 42

Skill 8.2 Interpreting Assessment Data 43

COMPETENCY 9.0 Understand how to use assessment and evaluation information and data to plan educational programs and school improvement 45

Skill 9.1 Using Assessment Data 45

Skill 9.2 Reporting Assessment Results to Students and Parents 46

TEACHER CERTIFICATION STUDY GUIDE

Subarea: **COUNSELING AND GROUP GUIDANCE**

COMPETENCY 10.0   Understand principles and techniques of individual counseling 49

Skill 10.1   The Scope of the School Counselor's Role 49

Skill 10.2   Major Counseling Theories and Approaches 51

Skill 10.3   Application of Counseling Theories and Techniques to a Specific Situation 70

COMPETENCY 11.0   Apply knowledge of group counseling principles and procedures 73

Skill 11.1   Merits and Limitations of Group Counseling 73

Skill 11.2   Group Dynamics 74

COMPETENCY 12.0   Apply knowledge of group guidance and principles 76

Skill 12.1   Developing Special Programs to Meet Identified Needs 76

Skill 12.2   Basic Prevention Concepts and Other Curricular Strategies 77

COMPETENCY 13.0   Understand referral procedures 79

Skill 13.1   Utilizing External Resources 79

COMPETENCY 14.0   Understand intervention procedures 81

Skill 14.1   Core Crisis Intervention Concepts and Approaches 81

Skill 14.2   The School Counselor as Advocate 83

TEACHER CERTIFICATION STUDY GUIDE

COMPETENCY 15.0 Understand the needs of students with special concerns (e.g., at-risk students, students with personal or family problems) 84

Skill 15.1 Child Abuse and Neglect 84

Skill 15.2 Substance Abuse and Addiction 85

Skill 15.3 Suicide, Self-Injury, Eating Disorders and Interpersonal Violence 86

COMPETENCY 16.0 Understand issues related to the needs of students from all cultural backgrounds 89

Skill 16.1 Cultural Competence 89

Skill 16.2 Bullying, Stereotyping and Prejudice 90

Skill 16.3 Aggression, Violence, and Conflict Resolution 91

Subarea: EDUCATIONAL AND CAREER PLANNING

COMPETENCY 17.0 Apply procedures for determining educational placement in relation to career goals 94

Skill 17.1 Educational Placement and Career Goals 94

COMPETENCY 18.0 Apply knowledge of approaches for and theories of career development and occupational choice 95

Skill 18.1 Similarities and Differences of Career Development Theories 95

COMPETENCY 19.0 Understand career development and career decision-making procedures 99

Skill 19.1 Strategies for Developing Employability Skills 99

Skill 19.2 Exploring Education and Career Options 100

Skill 19.3 Evaluating and Identifying Educational and Vocational Materials 103

TEACHER CERTIFICATION STUDY GUIDE

COMPETENCY 20.0 Understand career development and information programs.. .... **107**

Skill 20.1 Decision Making and Career Development 107

Skill 20.2 Student Appraisal Data Relevant to Career Development 108

COMPETENCY 21.0 Understand postsecondary education planning **111**

Skill 21.1 Postsecondary Education Options 111

Skill 21.2 Locating and Securing Scholarship and Financial Aid Assistance 112

Subarea: GUIDANCE PROGRAMS AND PROFESSIONAL KNOWLEDGE

COMPETENCY 22.0 Apply procedures for determining and reporting comprehensive guidance and counseling program needs, priorities, and objectives **114**

Skill 22.1 Needs Assessment and Program Evaluation Techniques 114

Skill 22.2 Developing Objectives and Determining Outcomes Based on Data 116

COMPETENCY 23.0 Apply knowledge of professional responsibilities, standards, and issues related to school counselors **119**

Skill 23.1 Professional Standards of the American School Counseling Association (ASCA) and American Counseling Association (ACA) 119

Skill 23.2 Professional Development 121

COMPETENCY 24.0 Understand the structure and functions of the Michigan Comprehensive Guidance and Counseling Program **123**

Skill 24.1 Michigan's Comprehensive Guidance and Counseling Program 123

GUIDANCE COUNSELOR

TEACHER CERTIFICATION STUDY GUIDE

COMPETENCY 25.0 Apply consultation, collaboration, and coordination procedures **125**

Skill 25.1 Components of a Consultation Model 125

Skill 25.2 Strategies for Effective Collaboration 128

COMPETENCY 26.0 Understand principles and procedures for establishing and maintaining effective school-home relationships **131**

Skill 26.1 Parents and Guardians as Partners 131

Skill 26.2 Knowledge of Family Dynamics 133

Skill 26.3 Conducting an Orientation Program to the School and Guidance Program 135

COMPETENCY 27.0 Apply knowledge of legal and ethical issues related to the rights and responsibilities of students, parents and guardians, and school personnel **136**

Skill 27.1 Legal Rights of Students and Parents Concerning Student Records and Assessment Data 136

Skill 27.2 Legislation Regarding Exceptional Students 137

Skill 27.3 Laws Regarding Child Abuse and Neglect 139

BIBLIOGRAPHY **142**

SAMPLE TEST **145**

ANSWER KEY **180**

RIGOR TABLE **181**

ANSWER RATIONALES **182**

TEACHER CERTIFICATION STUDY GUIDE

Great Study and Testing Tips!

What to study in order to prepare for the subject assessments is the focus of this study guide but equally important is *how* you study.

You can increase your chances of truly mastering the information by taking some simple yet effective steps.

Study Tips:

1. Some foods aid the learning process.

Foods such as milk, nuts, seeds, rice, and oats help your study efforts by releasing natural memory enhancers called CCKs (*cholecystokinin*) composed of *tryptopha*n, *choline* and *phenylalanine*. All of these chemicals enhance the neurotransmitters associated with memory.

Before studying, try a light, protein-rich meal of eggs, turkey or fish. All of these foods release memory-enhancing chemicals. The better the connections in your brain, the more you comprehend. Likewise, before you take a test, stick to a light snack of energy-boosting and relaxing foods. A glass of milk, a piece of fruit, or some peanuts all contain CCKs and help you to relax and focus on the subject at hand.

2. Learn to take great notes.

We learn best when information is organized. When it has a logical structure and we can see relationships between pieces of information helps us assimilate new information.

If your notes are scrawled all over the paper, it fragments the flow of the information. Instead, strive for clarity. Newspapers, for example, use a standard format to achieve clarity. Your notes can be much clearer through use of proper formatting. A very effective format is called the *"Cornell Method."*

> Take a sheet of loose-leaf lined notebook paper and draw a line all the way down the paper about 1-2" from the left-hand edge.
>
> Draw another line across the width of the paper about 1-2" up from the bottom. Repeat this process on the reverse side of the page.

Look at the highly effective result. You have ample room for notes, a left hand margin for special emphasis items or inserting supplementary data from the textbook, a large area at the bottom for a brief summary, and a little rectangular space for just about anything you want.

GUIDANCE COUNSELOR

3. Get the concept and then the details.

Too often we focus on the details and don't grasp an understanding of the concept. However, if you simply memorize only dates, places, or names, you may well miss the whole point of the subject.

A key way to understand things is to put them in your own words. If you are working from a textbook, automatically summarize each paragraph in your mind. If you are outlining text, don't simply copy the author's words.

Rephrase them in your own words. You remember your own thoughts and words much better than someone else's, and will subconsciously tend to associate the important details to the core concepts.

4. Ask why.

Pull apart written material paragraph by paragraph – and don't forget the captions under the illustrations.

If you train your mind to think in a series of questions and answers, not only will you learn more, but you will also have less test anxiety because you are used to answering questions.

Example: If the heading is "Stream Erosion", flip it around to read "Why do streams erode?" Then answer the questions.

5. Read for reinforcement and future needs.

Even if you only have 10 minutes, put your notes or a book in your hand. Your mind is similar to a computer; you have to input data in order to have it processed. *By reading, you are creating the neural connections for future retrieval.* The more times you read something, the more you reinforce the learning of ideas.

Even if you don't fully understand something on the first pass, *your mind stores much of the material for later recall.*

6. Relax to learn: in other words, go into exile.

Our bodies respond to an inner clock called biorhythms. Burning the midnight oil works well for some people, but not others.

If possible, set aside a particular place to study that is free of distractions. Shut off the television, cell phone and pager, and exile your friends and family during your study period.

If you really are bothered by silence, try background music. Light classical music at a low volume has been shown to aid in concentration over other types of music. Music that evokes pleasant emotions without lyrics is highly suggested. Try just about anything by Mozart. It can relax you.

7. Use arrows not highlighters.

At best, it's difficult to read a page full of yellow, pink, blue, and green streaks. Try staring at a neon sign for a while and you'll soon see that the horde of colors obscures the message.

A quick note, a brief dash of color, an underline or an arrow pointing to a particular passage is much clearer than a cascade of highlighted words.

8. Budget your study time.

Although you shouldn't ignore any of the material, *allocate your available study time in the same ratio that topics may appear on the test.* In other words, focus on the areas that are most likely to be included in the test.

TEACHER CERTIFICATION STUDY GUIDE

Testing Tips:

1. Get smart by playing dumb. Don't read anything into the question.

Don't make an assumption that the test writer is looking for something other than what is asked. Stick to the question as written and don't read anything into it.

2. Read the question and all the choices *twice* before answering the question.

You may miss something by not carefully reading, and then re-reading both the question and the answers.

If you really don't have a clue as to the right answer, leave it blank on the first time through. Go on to the other questions, as they may provide a clue as to how to answer the skipped questions.

If later on, you still can't answer the skipped ones . . . **Guess.** The only penalty for guessing is that you *might* get it wrong. One thing is certain; if you don't put anything down, you will get it wrong!

3. Turn the question into a statement.

Look at the way the questions are worded. The syntax of the question usually provides a clue. Does it seem more familiar as a statement rather than as a question? Does it sound strange?

By turning a question into a statement, you may be able to spot if an answer sounds right, and it may also trigger memories of material you have read.

4. Look for hidden clues.

It's actually very difficult to compose multiple-foil (choice) questions without giving away part of the answer in the options presented.

In most multiple-choice questions, you can often readily eliminate one or two of the potential answers. This leaves you with only two real possibilities and automatically your odds go to fifty-fifty with very little work.

TEACHER CERTIFICATION STUDY GUIDE

5. Trust your instincts.

For every fact you have read, you subconsciously retain something of that knowledge. On questions that you aren't really certain about, go with your basic instincts. **Your first impression on how to answer a question is usually correct.**

6. Mark your answers directly on the test booklet.

Don't bother trying to fill in the optical scan sheet on the first pass through the test. *Just be very careful not to miss-mark your answers when you eventually transcribe them to the scan sheet.*

7. Watch the clock!

You have a set amount of time to answer the questions. Don't get bogged down trying to answer a single question at the expense of 10 questions you can answer more readily.

THIS PAGE BLANK

TEACHER CERTIFICATION STUDY GUIDE

Subarea: HUMAN DEVELOPMENT AND LEARNING

COMPETENCY 1.0 Understand human development from early childhood to adulthood

SKILL 1.1   Major Theories of Social and Personality Development

There are many theories in the literature of human and personality development as well as in counseling and psychotherapy. The major theories explored in this section are psychoanalytic theory (as created by Freud and developed by his followers) and the related psychodynamic models of Erikson and Adler, and behaviorism. In subsequent sections, we address theories of cognitive development (see Skill 4.1) and other theories of counseling and behavior change such as existential, person-centered, Gestalt, cognitive-behavioral, reality, and solution-focused therapies (see Skill 10.2).

PSYCHOANALYTIC THEORY

The basis of many theories of psychology and counseling is the psychoanalytic theory of **Sigmund Freud**. Others who embraced psychoanalytic theory were Otto Rank, Heinz Hartman, Ernest Jones, Anna Freud, Alfred Adler, Heinz Kohut, Erik Erikson, Carl Jung, Karen Horney, Harry Stack Sullivan, John Bowlby, Margaret Mahler, Jacques Lacan, and Nancy Chodorow. Many broadened Freud's original ideas into different schools; these are often collectively referred to as psychodynamic theory and therapy.

Freud viewed human behavior as primarily the manifestation of biological and instinctive drives, unconscious motivation, and irrational forces. He divided the personality into the following parts:

- the ID, the part of the personality that is blind, demanding, pleasure-seeking and insistent; its function is to lessen tension and to return the psyche to a sense of homoeostasis or status quo;
- the EGO, the part of the personality that is the arbitrator between external reality and internal impulses and experiences; and
- the SUPER EGO, the part of the personality representing moral training whose goal is perfection and "doing the right thing".

He also explored the concept of the unconscious by using techniques of dream analysis, post-hypnotic suggestion, and free association. Anxiety and various ego-defense mechanisms were other components of the personality.

Psychoanalytic therapy aims to reconstruct the personality instead of solving immediate problems, with a focus on the past in order to analyze aspects of the unconscious that affect present behavior. Goals for clients include insight into their unconscious psychodynamics, greater ability to understand the connection between their past and present behaviors, and more psychological awareness. According to psychoanalytic theory, there are five stages of psychosexual development. These stages are:

1. **Oral** - The mouth is the source of satisfaction - If these oral needs are not met, greediness and acquisitiveness may develop as well as the rejection of others' love, fear of intimate relationships, and mistrust of others.

2. **Anal** - Control of the feces is the source of satisfaction - Negative feelings, including rage, hatred, destructiveness and hostility, are experienced if the need to control one's own bodily functions is not successfully resolved.

3. **Phallic** - The phallus (penis/clitoris) are the source of satisfaction - Penis envy and castration anxiety are associated with this stage of development. Resolution of sexual conflicts and sex-role identity is a critical task at this stage with the Electra and Oedipus complexes resulting from difficulties associated with this stage.

4. **Latency** – This stage has been thought to be a relatively calm period of inward and self-centered preoccupation. If not resolved adequately, narcissistic orientation can occur. The latency period usually occurs between the ages of 5 and 12.

5. **Genital** - This stage is signaled by physical maturity. Preoccupation with the sex organs is possible if not adequately resolved.

Psychopathology results from failing to meet one or more critical developmental tasks or becoming fixated at an early level of development. Neurotic personality development is regarded as an incomplete resolution of one of the stages of psychosexual development. Behavior is determined by unconscious forces, early experiences, and sexual and aggressive impetus.

Projection of the client's feelings upon the therapist is used to facilitate therapy; this is called *transference*. To enhance this process, the therapist tries to remain a "blank slate."

Other techniques used in this therapy include:

1. **Maintaining the Analytic Framework** – The therapist strives to adhere to strict relational rules, including nondisclosure on the part of the therapist/analyst, utilizing psychoanalytic techniques maintaining the contractual agreement for payment of fees, and having sessions regularly and consistently.

2. **Free Association** -This technique encourages the client to say whatever comes to mind in order to reveal the unconscious and give the therapist the opportunity to interpret the unconscious thoughts.

3. **Interpretation** – This is the process of analyzing the material the client reveals from the unconscious via free association and dreams.

4. **Dream Analysis** – This process encourages clients to report and discuss their dreams. The client is then encouraged by the therapist to free associate to various parts of and symbols contained in the dream. The analyst offers interpretations.

5. **Analysis and Interpretation of Resistance** – This technique involves an analysis of the ways the client is resisting the process of change.

6. **Analysis and Interpretation of Transference** – In this approach, the therapist interprets and discusses the significance of the transference process and the therapist-client relationship.

Subsequent developments in psychoanalytic theory that are considered "psychodynamic" are still grounded in key concepts from psychoanalytic theory. These include the role of the unconscious in conscious functioning, the relationship between childhood experiences and adult behavior, a developmental framework of personality, and some of the elements of the therapy process.

However, many of these offshoots are more likely to incorporate ideas about the role of external factors such as other people, the environment, and social norms in the development of personality as well as intervention. These theorists focus upon the ego and its development, as well as the development of the self as an individual.

The goal of these theories is to help the client become more aware of the unconscious, as well as to strengthen the ego system so behavior is based upon reality. Psychodynamic theories include **ego psychology**, **object relations**, **attachment theory**, **psychosocial theory**, **analytical psychology**, and **interpersonal therapy.**

Margaret Mahler was instrumental in developing the object relations theory of psychoanalysis. This theory focuses upon predetermined stages of development in which the child focuses less and less upon self and begins to see the world in relation to others. As development progresses, the child transitions from:

1. "**normal infantile autism**" - where the infant responds to physical stress, does not see a unified self, and considers self and mother as one; to a

2. "**symbiotic relationship**" - with the mother from 1-2 months of age, where the infant is dependent upon the mother and expects emotional congruence with the mother (mother also benefits from the relationship); to a

3. "**separation from this symbiotic relationship**" which occurs as the child gains cognitive awareness of being a separate person around 16-18 months of age; to becoming

4. "**individualized**", a process that takes place from age 18 months to approximately 3 years of age, and finally; into the

5. "**integration of self**" or maturation as a 3-1/2 – 4 year old.

If a trauma occurs during the separation-individuation phase, borderline and narcissistic personalities often develop; in other words, people often have difficulty with regulating their sense of self and their relationships with others.

More recently, **interpersonal therapy** has emerged from psychoanalytic theories. This time-limited approach also incorporates concepts and structure from cognitive-behavioral therapy and other intervention approaches. It is commonly used with people experiencing depression.

A structural overview of the various concepts and schools of thought in psychoanalytic and psychodynamic theory can be found at en.wikipedia.org/wiki/Psychoanalysis.

Contributions of psychoanalytic theory are:
1. This theory is the basis for all psychological theorizing involved in the explanation of human behavior, because it was the first theory.

2. The approach provides a framework for exploring an individual's history and their relationship to the present by way of the unconscious

3. The concept of resolving resistance to the change process is a key aspect of the success of the therapeutic process.

4. Many of the techniques of the therapy can be applied to other therapeutic Models, including the development of interpersonal therapy.

Limitations of the theory include:

1. For people utilizing traditional psychoanalytic therapy, a prolonged therapist training period is required. Further, work with clients also tends to be long-term.

2. The importance of action to alleviate the problem is not recognized.

3. The basic concepts of the theory are not verifiable by empirical research.

4. The theory is based on neurotic rather than healthy personalities.

5. The theory cannot be used in crisis counseling where immediate solutions are needed.

6. Traditional psychoanalytic theory does not take into account social, cultural, and interpersonal variables, although some of the derivative schools of thought in psychodynamic theory do.

Some of the key vocabulary terms used in psychoanalytic and psychodynamic therapy are:

Abreaction - the emotional reliving of past painful experiences.

Anxiety - the result of repressing threatening thoughts or feelings.

Borderline Personality Disorder - the pathology that develops when an individual fails to adequately develop in the separation-individuation phase, characterized by instability, irritability, self-destruction, impulsive anger, and extreme mood shifts.

Compensation - an ego defense mechanism that helps develop positive traits to make up for individual limitations.

Countertransference - a reaction towards the client by the therapist that can interfere with objectivity. It is generally related to the unmet and sometimes unconscious needs of the therapist.

Denial - the distortion of reality in an attempt to avoid dealing with a particular situation.

Displacement - the tendency to point ones' energy toward another person or object in order to reduce ones' own anxiety.

Ego - the part of the personality that mediates between the unconscious instincts and the environment.

Ego-Defense Mechanism - the unconscious process that operate to protect the individual from threatening and anxiety producing thoughts, feelings, and impulses. Examples include displacement, denial, repression and rationalization.

Ego Psychology – a theory of ego development reflecting different stages of life; formulated by Heinz Hartmann, Erik Erikson and other theorists.

Electra Complex - the unconscious sexual feelings of a daughter toward her father coupled with hostility toward her mother.

Free Association - the technique of permitting the client to say whatever comes to mind without censor.

Fixation - the process of getting stuck at a particular stage of psychosexual development.

Id - the part of the personality that is ruled by the pleasure principle. It is the center of the instincts, which are largely unconscious.

Interpretation - a technique of the therapist to explain a particular event or behavior.

Interjection - an ego defense mechanism where the client takes on behavior learned from another.

Libido - the energy of all life instincts including sexual energy.

Narcissistic Personality Disorder - a personality disorder characterized by extreme self-love, an exaggerated sense of self-importance, and an explosive attitude towards others; these attitudes usually hide a poor self-concept.

Object Relations – the theory that describes the interactional system of self and other; this theory is strongly based in developmental concepts.

Oedipus Complex - the unconscious sexual feelings of a son toward his mother coupled with hostility towards his father.

Projection - the tendency on the part of the client to attribute to others the qualities that are unacceptable in his/her own personality.

Psychic Energy - the drive that propels a person's behavior and psychological unctioning.

Rationalization - the method of explaining failures or negative occurrences.

Reaction Formation - an ego defense mechanism where a client strives to hide a socially unacceptable thought or feeling with behavior that is considered appropriate.

Regression - an ego defense mechanism of reverting to a less mature stage of development.

Repression - the unconscious act of pushing unacceptable or painful experiences into the unconscious.

Resistance - the client's unwillingness to share feelings and thoughts, or to make changes, in order for the psychoanalytic process to be successful.

Sublimation - the process of redirecting sexual and other biological energies into socially acceptable and creative avenues.

Super Ego - the part of the personality that determines what is right and wrong and strives to "be good."

Symbiosis - a relationship between two individuals that is advantageous or necessary to both. If an individual does not progress beyond this stage, borderline personality disorder can develop.

Transference - the fostering of emotions originally experienced towards one individual upon another individual not connected with the original experience (usually the therapist).

Working Through - the process of exploring unconscious material, ego defenses, transference, and resistance.

ERIKSON'S PSYCHOSOCIAL THEORY OF HUMAN DEVELOPMENT

Erik Erikson built on Freud's work and developed what is referred to as psychosocial theory. It focuses on developmental tasks in relation to self and others. The eight stages of life articulated in this theory are:

1. **Basic Trust vs. Basic Mistrust** – (Birth to approximately 18 months of age). The infant's needs for nourishment and care are satisfied. The response to these needs must be consistent so the infant develops a sense of trust and attachment to one or two adults. Mistrust results if the infant's needs are not met.

2. **Autonomy vs. Shame and Doubt** – (18 to 30 months of age). The child develops an early sense of independence and a measure of some control over the environment. This independence is manifested by self-feeding, dressing, toileting, etc. In this stage the child needs reassurance and support from the adults around him or her Overprotection should be avoided.

3. **Initiative vs. Guilt** – (2-1/2 to 5 years of age). The child develops an imagination and enjoys play-acting adult roles. The child is also learning to perform adult roles and begins to realize restraints are necessary. A pervasive sense of guilt occurs if the child is not successful in initiating everyday activities and tasks.

4. **Industry vs. Inferiority** – (Elementary and middle school years). The child becomes curious with the need to explore and manipulate the environment around her or him. Competency is reached through accomplishments. The child becomes increasingly aware of interactions with others in the school and neighborhood. If a sense of adequacy is not acquired during this stage, feelings of inferiority occur.

5. **Identity vs. Role Confusion** – (Adolescence). The child is striving for an identity and sense of self-worth. Adolescents seek to formulate their own values, beliefs and style of life. They experiment with different lifestyles. If previous stages have not been resolved satisfactorily, the tasks may reoccur here as developmental problems. Resolving unfinished business is one of the major tasks of adolescence.

6. **Intimacy vs. Isolation** - This struggle occurs during young adulthood. The adult becomes willing to be open about self and to commit to a close personal relationship.

7. **Generativity vs. Stagnation** - Maturity is achieved. The task here is to establish and guide the next generation and come to terms with one's dreams and accomplishments.

8. **Ego-Integrity vs. Despair** - This stage occurs during later life. Despair may be experienced by the elderly if ego-integrity is not obtained. When successful, people have a sense of fulfillment about their lives.

ADLERIAN THEORY

Alfred Adler was originally a follower of Freud. Subsequent Adlerians include **Rudolf Dreikers** and **Harold Mosak**. Rudolf Dreikers was instrumental in applying Adlerian principles to group work. Where Freud explored the psychosexual aspects of personality, Adler concentrated upon the psychosocial aspects of human nature. He believed that people are in control of their lives, thus creating an individual lifestyle at an early age.

Adler called his approach *individual psychology*. In contrast to Freud, Adler felt that consciousness rather than unconsciousness was the core of personality theory. He did not believe in reliving childhood experiences, but instead using these early recollections as clues to understanding the lifestyle of the individual. Adler emphasized the positive abilities of the individual as influenced by societal forces and the capacity of each to reach optimal development. His theory became the basis for the ensuing humanistic theories that abound today. The main goal is confronting basic mistakes and assumptions the client has made and attempting to redirect them. The focus is on examining the beliefs of the client as expressed by his/her behavior.

Some key concepts in Adler's theory are:

- Childhood experiences are not as crucial in themselves as is the attitude toward these experiences.
- All people have a unique lifestyle, none of which are the same.
- One's lifestyle is set by age 5 and is a reaction to perceived inferiority.
- One's lifestyle is learned from early family interactions.
- Behavior is motivated by social needs and has a goal oriented direction.

For more information about Adlerian psychotherapy, go to ourworld.compuserve.com/homepages/hstein/.

Contributions of Adler's theory are:

1. The theory was a major impetus for the development of other humanistic theories.

2. The theory has influenced cognitive-behavioral theories, family therapies, and general mental health work. Currently, it is impacting emerging theories of culturally competent counseling.

The limitations of the theory are:

1. An inability to validate the vaguely defined concepts with empirical data.

2. The oversimplification of complex human functioning.

3. It is based too heavily on a common sense perspective.

Key terms of Adlerian thought are:

Avoiding traps - the therapist's efforts to avoid reinforcing clients' destructive behavior patterns.

Basic Mistakes - self-defeating beliefs (such as an extreme need for security, unattainable goals and doubting one's worth) which influence the formation of one's personality.

Catching oneself - the process of the client to become more aware of self-destructive behavior, irrational thoughts, and the anticipation of events before they happen.

Convictions - the results of life experiences.

Courage - the ability to take risks.

Encouragement - the process used in therapy to help clients reach realistic goals by using all their resources, recognizing their positive traits and transforming negative traits into positive assets.

Family Constellations - "pictures" of family dynamics and relationships.

Fictional Finalism - the ideal image one sees oneself becoming; one's ultimate goal.

Holism - the viewing of one's personality as a whole.

Immediacy - dealing with the present moment in the counseling process.

Individual Psychology - the uniqueness and unity of the individual.

Individuality - the way we develop our own style of striving for competence.

Inferiority Feelings - the negative feeling one has about oneself. These feelings can be both real and imagined.

Life Tasks - the life work of all humans to attain a satisfying lifestyle.

Lifestyle - the way in which one perceives life and upon which the personality is formed.

Motivational Modification - the therapist's interest in helping clients to want to change their' negative lifestyle goals and challenging their basic negative concepts.

Paradoxical Intention - the technique that is characterized by helping the client invoke exaggerated debilitating thoughts and behaviors, helping the client accept and conquer his/her resistance, thus becoming more aware of his/her behavior and being responsible for the consequences of that behavior.

Phenomenological Orientation - the technique of the therapist that attempts to view the world from the client's point of view.

Priorities - a coping method used to obtain satisfaction in life. By pointing out a client's priorities the therapist hopes to help the client realize the feelings invoked in others and the price the client pays by clinging to these negative priorities.

Private Logic - the central psychological framework of the client; the philosophy upon which one bases one's lifestyle, including basic mistakes and faulty assumptions that often do not conform to reality.

Push-Button - a technique that teaches the client that he/she can control and their thoughts and feelings.

Social Interest - the attitude a client has regarding society; a sense of empathy and identification with the larger community.

Spitting in the Client's Soup - a technique that reduces the usefulness of a client's manipulative behavior. By pointing out the manipulation, the therapist effectively defeats the client's anticipated results of the manipulation.

Striving for Superiority - the desire to become competent and perfect; also known as the "**growth force**".

Task Setting and Commitment - the technique taught to the client to formulate realistic, attainable goals that can be revised if necessary.

BEHAVIORISM

The behavioral theories of psychological development and therapy that developed in the 1950s and 1960s were a radical protest to the psychoanalytic theories that had held sway for many years. The key figures in behaviorism were **Arnold Lazarus**, **Albert Bandura**, **Joseph Wolpe** and **Alan Kazdin**. They built on the work of learning theorists (see Skill 1.2). Contemporary behavior therapy utilizes many concepts, research methods, and treatments to account for and change behavior. In contrast to the psychoanalytic theories, behavior therapies are focused on current behavior as well as methods to change self-destructive behaviors.

Behavior theory describes the principles of learned behavior. The main goal of behavior therapy is to eliminate negative learned behaviors or self-defeating behaviors by having the client learn new, more effective and positive ways of dealing with situations that create behavior problems. The client and the therapist work together to formulate goals. In this process, they detail specific methods to address the client's self-defeating behavior. The client must have a sense of ownership regarding the goals in order to make them work.

The job of the therapist in behavior therapy is to

- make the problem clear,
- verbalize the consequences of the behavior manifested by the client,
- serve as a role model for the client,
- help formulate alternative courses of action with possible consequences,
- advocate behavior change, and provide reinforcement to the client when the behavior changes.

There should be an objective assessment of the results of the therapy. The job of the client is to help the therapist explore the alternatives to the problematic behavior, be open to trying new strategies and be willing to take the risk of trying these new strategies outside the therapeutic session.

Although the goals of the therapy are specific and concrete, and the problems are defined, the procedures and techniques of the therapy are contingent upon the needs of each client. Therefore no set of specific techniques is used, although some methods are used more often than others. Some of these methods are relaxation, systematic desensitization, reinforcement, modeling, assertive training, multimodal therapy and self-management programs. Therapy should focus on behavior change, not on attitude change, and actions are expected to follow verbalization (in other words, practice in real life).

Contributions of behavior theory and therapy are:

1. The techniques are based upon empirical research. Any technique that is not effective empirically is discarded.

2. Treatment is based upon the assessment of individual needs.

3. The therapy is effective in the short-term, yielding results that can be widely applied.

4. The approaches can be used with culturally diverse client populations because of the emphasis on teaching the client about the process and the structure of the therapy.

Some of the limitations of the therapy are:

1. Success depends upon the ability to control environmental factors.

2. In institutional settings, there is a danger of imposing conformity at the expense of individual needs.

3. The therapy does not address philosophical human problems such as values and identity issues.

4. The therapist can, if desired, direct a client towards the goals of the therapist instead of the goals of the client. This may be especially true if the therapist does not agree with the client's value system.

5. Past history is not an important factor in the therapy, therefore the assumption is that past experiences and childhood traumatic events do not play a role in present behaviors.

Key terms in *behaviorism* are:

Assertive Training - Teaching skills and techniques for dealing with difficult situations in ways that are direct, firm and clear. Assertive training often challenges beliefs that accompany a lack of assertiveness and employs the technique of rehearsal.

Basic ID - an acronym for the seven major areas of personality functioning: **b**ehavior, **a**ffect, **s**ensations, **i**magery, **c**ognition, **i**nterpersonal and **d**rugs/biology. (Lazarus, 1981)

Behavior Rehearsal - a technique of trying out new behavioral approaches that can be used in real life situations.

Coaching - providing clients with general principles of how to make effective behavioral changes.

Cognitive Restructuring - the process of identifying and understanding the impact of negative behavior and thoughts, as well as learning to replace them with more realistic and appropriate actions and beliefs.

Contingency Contracting - the specific delineation of behavior to be performed, changed or discontinued, along with the rewards for the performance of these contractual items, the conditions under which these rewards are to be received, and the time limit involved.

Counterconditioning - the process of retraining problem behaviors and introducing new behaviors.

Feedback - the process of providing the client with verbal responses to behavior changes. The two parts of feedback are encouragement and praise for attempting the behavior change, and specific suggestions for making the behavior change work better.

Modeling - the process of showing new ways to do something. The therapist can help the client do this by role-playing the type of behavior that is desired. Albert Bandura has done much of the work in this area.

Multimodal Therapy - the process the therapist evokes in making an evaluation of the client's level of functioning at the beginning of the therapy, and subsequently adjusting procedures and techniques to the goals of the client. The behavior change is a function of techniques, strategies and modeling. Arnold Lazarus developed this type of therapy.

Negative Reinforcement - when the removal of an aversive stimulus is likely to increase a problem behavior.

Operant Conditioning - a concept from B.F. Skinner (a learning theorist) that says behaviors of an active organism are controlled and controllable, even without actual consequences each time.

Positive Reinforcement - a conditioning technique where an individual receives a desirable result for a positive behavior that subsequently increases the probability of that behavior reoccurring.

Progressive Relaxation - a technique employed to increase the ability of the client to control his/her stress level by gradually having the client relax.

Reinforcement - a specific response to a behavior that increases the probability of that behavior being repeated.

Self-Instructional Training/Management - strategies used to teach coping skills in problem situations such as anxiety, depression, and pain. Realistic goals are set and constantly evaluated. The consistent use of a particular strategy is essential, and support systems are important as are the use of self-reinforcement in order to achieve success.

Self-Monitoring - the process of observing one's behavior patterns and interactions in social situations.

Social Learning Theory - a theory originated by Alfred Bandura. The theory holds that behavior is understood by taking into consideration the social conditions under which learning occurs as well as individual psychological factors.

Systematic Desensitization - the process of teaching a client to become less sensitized to a particular stimulus, thereby reducing anxiety. The techniques consist of relaxation exercises combined with an imagined series of progressively more anxiety-producing situations. It was developed by Joseph Wolpe and is based upon the principles of classical conditioning.

Technical Eclecticism - the process of using different techniques from different therapies to achieve behavior change; the results is; flexibility in the therapeutic process.

SKILL 1.2 Basic Milestones in Physical, Motor and Language Development

The majority of changes in physical and motor growth and the development of language occur prior to five years of age. The primary exception to this is the transition at preadolescence (approximately ages 9-12) into puberty. Hormonal shifts and ongoing physical growth become acute at preadolescence and bring children into adolescence and physical maturity.

Language development in elementary school proceeds primarily in terms of the development of vocabulary and increased sophistication in the use of words and concepts.

The key physical and motor developmental milestones for school-age children and adolescents are noted below.

Ages 6-8:

- Growth slows but remains steady.
- Body proportions change, with legs getting longer.
- Less body fat and more muscle develops, with an increase in overall strength.
- Fine motor skills are enhanced, though muscle coordination is still uneven. This results in the ability to write in cursive in addition to the ability to print.
- Permanent teeth come in, sometimes causing crowding if the mouth has not developed enough.

Ages 9-12:

- Significant body changes as puberty approaches: weight gain, pubic and body hair, increased sweating, oily skin, genital development.
- Some children experience joint pain as a result of growth spurts.
- Girls generally develop sooner: their hips widen, breasts start to emerge, menstruation begins.
- Boys enter preadolescence later and their growth changes last longer.

Ages 13-17:

- Puberty is reached; the adolescent is physically mature.
- Girls reach their adult height by age 17; boys continue to add height into their 20s.

The following websites provide detailed information about developmental milestones and changes: **www.ces.ncsu.edu/depts/fcs/human.html**, **www.littleab.com/ABcare/develoment.html**, and **www.education.com/reference/ontrack/**.

COMPETENCY 2.0 Understand ways in which developmental stages and external factors affect educational counseling and assessment

Skill 2.1 The Impact of Stress on School Performance and Students' Well-being

Students' academic performance and behavior is impacted by a range of external factors as well as the students' developmental growth path. In subsequent sections of this study guide, we will address some of the issues affecting students at school as well as in their lives outside the school. These include exceptional educational needs, stereotyping and prejudice, bullying, violence, substance abuse, mental health problems and family issues, among others. These circumstances, characteristics and events can all be considered stressors on students.

Development as Stress

The normal challenges of developmental change can also function as stressors in a child's life. As children grow, experience hormonal shifts, increase their skill base, and gradually shift from a focus on family to peers and then to the larger world, they may experience the stress that often accompanies change. Some children seem to move easily from one stage to another; others feel each developmental shift acutely. Some experience generalized anxiety, revert to earlier levels of functioning for a short time, or become clingy and demanding. They may avoid opportunities for new friends, skill development, or extracurricular activities.

It is important for counselors to have an awareness of the range of reactions to developmental change. These responses can be the primary factor underlying difficulties in peer relationships or academic performance. Considering the role of development in each child's experience is crucial to addressing student needs and concerns effectively.

Impact on School Performance

Stressors can negatively impact academic achievement by making it difficult for the student to focus on learning. When a student is homeless, for example, it may be difficult for him or her to attend in class because of lack of sleep, worry about what is happening with a parent, or concerns about where dinner is coming from and other pressing life issues. Similarly, if a child is being abused at home, he or she may have difficulties with attention and focus.

Some stressors, such as medical conditions, may prevent a child from participating in some school activities or require homebound instruction. While accommodations need to be made for alternative programming, the inability to be "part of the group" still may impair peer relationships and affect skill development and motivation.

Stressors can also have a less direct impact. A challenging home life may make it hard for a student to complete homework assignments or study effectively. Chronic stress and traumatic events also contribute to a lack of self confidence, poor motivation, inadequate social skills, depression, anxiety, and other mental health problems. These difficulties may interfere with a student's ability to participate effectively in the school environment. They can also disrupt the student's efforts to study and do homework.

Individuality and Resiliency

Individuals respond in different ways to the same or similar stressors, and the impact of such stressors needs to be assessed for each student. Mitigating factors include coping skills, personality traits, prior experience with stress and trauma, the degree of social isolation created by the stressful event(s), the quality of attachment to and presence of significant adults in the student's life, and the amount and kind of support the student receives in relation to the stressor.

Resiliency is the ability to thrive in spite of difficult circumstances. Research suggests that several of the most important factors in building resiliency are the presence of a caring, competent adult in the child's life, an attitude of hope and interest in life, and good problem solving skills. Helping students identify or find an important adult upon whom they can rely, teaching problem solving and coping skills, and discussing ways to think about what life brings to us are all good strategies for helping students become more resilient. This, in turn, enhances their well-being as well as their capacity for academic and vocational achievement.

Skill 2.2   Developmental Variations

Any given child's developmental path is not as tidy and consistent as theory and therefore does not always fit into ordered patterns. This is an important concept when considering theories, stages and developmental milestones. Stage theories and lists of developmental milestones need to be considered markers to guide the observer, not absolute standards within which all children will neatly fit.

Physical, Genetic, Environmental and Cultural Effects on Development

The differences in children and their rate of development are influenced by the experiences they have and the environment or culture in which they live. Basic differences in caregiver style and availability, the quality of physical nutrition, and the presence or lack of trauma and violence in the environment all impact children's development. Socioeconomic status, gender, language acquisition, basic cognitive ability and heredity are other factors that influence children's development, behavior and their perspective on the world, as do ethnicity and race. Religion does not generally affect developmental growth, except to the extent that religious practices set the student apart from peers and therefore impact social development in the context of the larger world (outside of the religious group).

School counselors and other professionals need to be aware of developmental theories and milestones. Such knowledge provides a background against which they are better able to determine if a child or adolescent is developmentally delayed or needs assistance in reaching his or her full potential. However, the uniqueness of each individual should also be perceived and valued when assessing a particular child's developmental status.

Inclusion of students with special educational needs into the general education classroom is not only essential for advanced academic achievement but also for socio-cultural development. Researchers continue to show that personalized learning environments increase the learning effect for students, decrease drop-out rates among marginalized students, and decrease unproductive student behavior that can result from constant cultural misunderstandings or miscues between students.

TEACHER CERTIFICATION STUDY GUIDE

COMPETENCY 3.0 Understand characteristics of students with special educational needs

Skill 3.1 Specific Populations

Although every student has special needs because he or she is an individual, there are some students who, by virtue of birth or life circumstance, belong to a group with specific needs. Again, as noted previously, not all children and adolescents who belong to a certain group will necessarily fit a description or profile of group characteristics, because each student is an individual. For example, a particular girl may express a learning style more commonly associated with boys.

However, for the purpose of alerting school counselors to issues their students may face, these factors may be of concern to selected populations.

Migrant worker families:

- Chronic disruption in living circumstances and education, resulting in significant gaps in learning.
- Social isolation.
- Inadequate nutrition and medical care.
- Bias due to stereotyping.
- Stress due to the problems noted above as well as economic hardship.

Immigrant families and those for whom English is a second language:

- Loss of homeland and extended family.
- Difficulties with learning, socialization and peer group acceptance due to language limitations.
- Bias due to stereotyping.
- Post-traumatic stress due to precipitating events that prompted immigration and/or losses associated with relocation.

Homeless families:

- Multiple losses and traumas, and related post-traumatic stress.
- Disruption in living circumstances and education, resulting in significant gaps in learning.
- Inadequate nutrition, sleep and medical care.
- Underlying anxiety due to chaotic and/or unpredictable environment.
- Absenteeism for various reasons.

Families displaced due to catastrophic events (such as hurricanes):

- Multiple losses and traumas, and related post-traumatic stress.
- Disruption in living circumstances and education.
- Lack of social network and extended family support.
- Sudden change in economic circumstances.

Families living in poverty:

- Chronic stress due to economic hardship and challenging life circumstances.
- Inadequate resources for special events at school (field trips, testing, dances, sporting events, etc.).
- Inadequate nutrition and medical care.
- Absenteeism due to the need to attend to pressing family matters.

Gifted and talented students:

- Boredom, which may lead to behavior problems.
- Need for special services and/or creative programming.
- Bias due to stereotyping.

Learning support and special education students:

- Increased need for appropriate attention and support from faculty and staff.
- Specific accommodations during standardized testing situations.
- Need for evaluation, special services and/or creative programming.
- Bias due to stereotyping.

Emotional support students:

- Presence of significant mental health issues.
- Increased need for appropriate attention from faculty and staff, including consultation with other professionals, evaluation, referral, and follow-up.
- Specific accommodations during standardized testing situations.
- Need for special services and/or creative programming.
- Bias due to stereotyping.

Sensory-impaired students:

- Specific accommodations for various classroom activities, as well as during standardized testing situations.
- Increased need for consultation with other professionals, and, at times, need for evaluation, referral, and follow-up.
- Need for special services and/or creative programming.
- Bias due to stereotyping.

SKILL 3.2 Characteristics of Students with Cognitive Impairment

Students with cognitive impairments are one group of students with what are often called "exceptional" educational needs. Other students, as noted above, are those with social or emotional problems, sensory impairment, medical conditions, or learning disabilities. There are many different categories and diagnoses that may be utilized to describe these students. Though not detailed here, school counselors need to familiarize themselves with the needs of these students.

Traditionally, "special education" referred to students with cognitive impairment or "mental retardation." Cognitive impairments exist on a continuum and different students will need varying degrees of support and special programming. The basic characteristics of students with cognitive impairment fall into four categories linked largely to IQ scores.

Mild (IQ of 50-55 to 70)
- Delays in most areas (communication, motor, academic)
- Often not distinguished from normal children until of school age.
- Can acquire both academic and vocational skills; can become self-supporting

Moderate IQ of 35-40 to 50-55)
- Only fair motor development; clumsy
- Poor social awareness
- Can be taught to communicate
- Can profit from training in social and vocational skills; needs supervision, but can perform semiskilled labor as an adult

Severe (IQ of 20-25 to 35-40)
- Poor motor development
- Minimal speech and communication
- Minimal ability to profit from training in health and self-help skills: may contribute to self-maintenance under constant supervision as an adult

Profound (IQ below 20-25)
- Gross retardation, both mental and sensor-motor
- Little or no development of basic communication skills
- Dependency on others to maintain basic life functions
- Lifetime of complete supervision (institution, home, nursing home)

COMPETENCY 4.0 Understand principles of learning and motivation

Skill 4.1 Major Theories of Learning and Cognitive Development

Theories about learning are quite varied. Behaviorism (see Skill 1.1) describes much about how individuals learn, and many of the concepts of behaviorism are central to learning and cognitive development. The theorists in this area of study include the functionalists, the associationists and the cognitive developmentalists. (For an interesting description of various theories and models related to learning, see www.learning-theories.com/.)

The study of consciousness within the context of the environment, instead of studying consciousness as an isolated element, was the main contribution of functionalist theorists **Edward Thorndike**, **B.F. Skinner**, **John G. Watson** and **C.L. Hull** to learning theory. They opposed the introspective techniques of psychoanalytic approaches because it did not explore the relationship with other elements in the person's environment. The functionalists insisted that mental function be studied in relationship to the world surrounding the individual. Many of the ideas in behaviorism developed from this work.

Associationist theorists **Ivan Pavlov** and **William Estes** believed that experience or recall of one object builds upon and causes the recall of other objects related to or associated with that object. This is based on the theories of Aristotle. The key concept is that living organisms' responses to environmental stimuli are governed by the sensory, response, and central nervous systems which consist of innate circuitry and memories of past experiences. The response of organisms is therefore dependent upon associating past memories with present stimuli. This theory applied to learning explains how infants expand their sphere of knowledge.

Cognitive theorists **Jean Piaget**, **Edward Tolman**, **Albert Bandura** and **Donald Norman** assign a prominent role to mental processes. The process of learning depends upon information received and the processing of that information which in turn depends upon mental processes, past experiences or behaviors, and present environmental factors. The person, the environment and behavior are interdependent. Faulty cognitive processes develop from inaccurate perceptions, overgeneralization, or incomplete or erroneous information.

Jean Piaget focused on cognition from a developmental perspective. In his view, development is defined as *the adaptive, orderly, changes experienced by the human organism from birth to death*. The child grows cognitively, socially, physically, and morally, gradually and at different rates. These four different types of growth and development impact on the learning process and the behavior patterns of the child.

Piaget studied how we organize knowledge at different times in our lives. He identified four stages of cognitive development. These are:

1. Sensorimotor Stage - From birth to two years. Development is based upon reflex; information is gained through the senses; the child begins to understand the concept of permanence, and begins to develop *problem solving behavior* through trial and error.

2. Pre-operational Stage - From ages two to seven years. The child starts to develop the ability to share experiences with others, uses symbols and shows rudimentary logical mental operations. The child has yet to develop the concept of *conservation,* the ability to understand that certain properties of an object do not change even though their appearance has changed. The concept of *centration* is the child's logic at this stage. This is the ability to focus on only one aspect of the properties of an object and not being able to understand that an object can have multiple properties without inherently changing. *Reversibility* at this stage is the inability of the child to back up and rethink a problem. The child can only respond to perceived appearances.

3. Concrete Operational Stage - From ages seven to eleven. At this stage the child understands the concepts of conservation, centration, and reversibility; masters the operations of classification, the identification of characteristics and serialization, and is capable of inferences. The child can now respond to inferred reality or facts.

4. Formal Operational Stage - From ages eleven to adult. At this stage the child develops and refines the capability of abstract thinking, can deal with hypothetical situations and exercises higher order thinking such as synthesis and evaluation.

One limitation of Piaget's theory is the fact that he did not consider the effect of culture and the social environment on children's development. **Lev Vygotsky** was one theorist who approached cognitive development from a more social standpoint. He suggested that cognitive development started with social interactions and moved inward.

Current theories of cognitive development focus on the concept that humans develop according to various information processing mechanism that are specific to different areas of learning and growth. This is called domain specificity. These theorists argue that information processing is grounded in evolutionary adaptation. A leading proponent of this approach in relation to language acquisition is **Noam Chomsky**.

Skill 4.2 Learning Styles and Individual Differences

Human learning is a complex human behavior and the way one learns is as individual and unique as each person. Different styles refer to the *preference* a person may have for learning in a particular way; this approach does not suggest that students can only learn in that way. In fact, exposure to varied learning approaches can be beneficial and growth-enhancing.

Research into learning styles has yielded eighteen different elements that contribute to various learning styles. In an attempt to classify this information, **Dunn** and **Dunn** isolated four different learning styles with varying components. These learning styles take into consideration the varied aspects of the way individuals learn. Further, Dunn and Dunn have developed a learning style inventory that assesses each of these elements.

The four major aspects of learning styles and learning environments are:

Environmental Elements: There are four environment elements that affect the way a student learns. These elements are part of the learning style of the student.

The element of *sound* varies with the learning. Some children can block out sound completely when studying and learning; others require complete silence. Others need only relative quiet and while still others must have a familiar sound, such as music or television, to block out extraneous noises that interrupt their train of thought. Still others can concentrate with or without sound, in silence or noise, or with any sound at all.

Light is also a factor in learning but not as critical as the element of sound. Some students need intensely bright lights in order to be comfortable in reading or writing and consequently become drowsy and lethargic in inadequate light. Some students prefer a subdued light to feel comfortable.

Tolerance to *temperature* varies greatly according to the individual. Concentration alters with the need for warmth or coolness, which can affect the degree of productivity of an individual.

The *design* of the study area is often critical to individual learning styles. Some students need an informal setting such as the floor or an easy chair. Others require a more formal setting such as a table or hard chair in order to concentrate adequately and for others there is no need to take into account the design of the site in which they study.

Emotional Elements: The emotional elements involved in the way a student learns also impacts on the quantity and quality of work produced.

The *motivated* student comes to the task with enthusiasm and excitement, asks questions and goes beyond the requirements of the class to explore further related areas. The *unmotivated* student cannot take in too much at one time, needs short assignments and requires the experience of success to continue to achieve. The unmotivated student will often respond to an individualized program of choices, teaming, or self-evaluation.

The trait of *persistence* is the ability to find the answer to a problem no matter how difficult. Persistent students will use resources or other students for help before asking the teacher for answers. They will not give up but continue to work on a problem until it is solved. Other students, such as those with short attention spans, find it difficult to maintain interest in the subject, daydream, become irritated or disruptive, and do not continue to attempt to solve problems for any period of time. These students need to have rules and objectives set out clearly.

The emotionally mature student shows signs of *responsibility* for the completion of the task at hand without constant supervision. Students who have difficulty learning because of reading problems become easily discouraged and need different methods of receiving material. They may need taped instruction, games, small groups or a structured multi-sensory learning packet. Their different learning styles do not conform to the expected norms.

The student who needs *structure* must have specific rules for the completion of an assignment. These include time limits, restriction of options, and a specific way of responding. Different students need different amounts of structure depending upon the learning style and ability to make decisions. The motivated, responsible and persistent student needs little structure while the unmotivated student with learning problems needs the most structure to achieve success.

Sociological Elements: The ability to learn varies with the student depending upon the atmosphere and individuals involved in the teaching situation. Students can learn from different individuals at different times and in different settings. These settings include learning from *peers, by oneself, in pairs or teams, with an adult or teacher, and in a mixed group.* How students learn sociologically can be determined by allowing them to choose their own method of studying and completing assignments with monitoring by the teacher to check on progress.

Physical Elements: The senses of *seeing, hearing, smelling, feeling* and *touching* are instrumental in the way many individuals learn. Those who learn through *visual* senses can see images in their mind; those who learn through their *auditory* senses learn by listening to sounds; those who learn by the *tactile approach* must be able to touch and feel in order to understand and those who learn through their *kinesthetic* senses need to have actual experiences with the shapes and forms of letters and words. Many students learn from a combination of some or all of the elements discussed.

Other physical elements involved in the process of learning include, the taking of food breaks or *intake, the optimum time of day or night*, and *the ability to move around at will*. Adjustments for these learning styles will produce the ideal atmosphere for learning.

Multiple Intelligences

Another theorist in learning styles is **Howard Gardner**. He has developed the idea of multiple intelligences. He posits that there are eight different kinds of intelligence and that each person is more or less inclined to demonstrate each of these. While this theory has engendered some debate in the field of education, it has opened up an important discussion about how schools can better respond to the diversity of students' learning styles. A multiple intelligence survey is available to assess a student's approach to learning. (For more information, see www.infed.org/thinkers/gardner.htm.)

In addition to the Dunn & Dunn Inventory and Gardner's multiple intelligence test, there are other learning style and personality inventories that can help determine the style or combination of styles suited to individual students. These include the **Schmeck, Ribich, & Ramanaiah Inventory of Learning** Process for information processing preferences, the **Myers-Briggs Type Indicator** for personality preferences, and the **Kolb Learning Style Inventory**. The assessment of a student who is having problems learning might give the teacher direction as to useful methods for motivating and encouraging a particular student to succeed.

Gender Differences and Learning Styles

Recent research and some educational practices have recently focused on differences in the ways girls and boys learn and function in the school environment. There is some indication that, as a group, boys tend to be more competitive and individualistic in their approach to learning, whereas girls are more inclined to work cooperatively with others, are more social, and are more interested in understanding ideas than in assessing facts.

Perhaps the most important thing for school counselors to remember is that gender (or other aspect of social identity such as race and ethnicity, immigration status or social class) is only one variable among a range of variables that contribute to the unique development and capabilities of a given individual. Further, differences within a given group (such as girls or boys) are almost always greater than the differences between two such groups. In other words, there is great variation among any given group of students and a range of individual and social factors contribute to these differences. Paying attention to each student's individual needs is the best approach to facilitating academic success.

See www.maec.org/beyond.html#learn and www.aauw.org/research/genderWars.cfm for more information about gender differences in the school environment.

TEACHER CERTIFICATION STUDY GUIDE

COMPETENCY 5.0 Understand principles and methods for promoting cognitive development

Skill 5.1   Basic Concepts to Promote Cognitive Development

Fundamental to cognitive development are some key experiences: exposure to new information, opportunities to experiment with ideas and thinking, and chances to utilize information and ideas in new ways. Further, students need practice using what they learn, and they need useful feedback from others. New information should be incrementally linked to information they already have. School counselors, teachers and others can incorporate a range of experiences as they address issues or teach specific content to students in order to enhance overall cognitive development and encourage thinking processes.

Some of the approaches that encourage positive and healthy cognitive development include:

- Inviting students to participate in age-appropriate discussions about a variety of topics, issues, and current events.

- Encouraging students to share ideas and thoughts with adults.

- Providing opportunities for students to think independently and develop their own ideas.

- Helping students set their own goals, track their work and utilize a planner.

- Offering students a range of learning experiences, including collaborative projects with other students.

- Complimenting and praising students for well-thought-out decisions.

- Helping students re-evaluate poorly made decisions.

Skill 5.2   Study Skills

Actively teaching study skills to students can be effective in enhancing cognitive development as well. Some students naturally study well and others need help with focus and organization. Efficient ways of studying have been researched by psychologists and others; this research has yielded methods about studying that help students retain information and learn in a more organized manner. The following suggestions are the result of these experiments.

1. Make a schedule and stick to it. Study at a certain time each day.

2. Find a place that is comfortable, suits your individual learning style, and is consistently available and convenient.

3. Have all the materials needed in one place before starting work so study will not be interrupted.

4. Study every day in order to develop the habit of knowing how to study when it is really needed.

5. Keep an accurate and comprehensible notebook in case you need to refer to it.

6. Keep a careful record of assignments. Use a calendar for due dates of all projects.

7. Use short cut devices for retaining information such as flash cards, self-tests or "cover cards" which succinctly detail the material to be retained. Repeat the material orally.

8. Take good notes that list the main points of the material.

9. After learning the material, continue to study to "over-learn." This helps retain the material for a longer period of time.

10. Review frequently after learning the material for the first time.

COMPETENCY 6.0 Understand principles and methods for promoting social and personal development

Skill 6.1 Creating Positive School Environments

A fundamental task of all schools is to create a positive environment within which all students are respected and can thrive. The school counselor can be instrumental in facilitating the positive school environment. While this task cannot be achieved alone by the school counselor or the guidance department, counselors need to be alert to the ways in which positive school environments can be established, and, in many cases, can be instrumental in effecting the healthy social development of students.

Positive school environments share these qualities:

- Core values of respect, integrity, cooperation and care for one another.

- Adults strive to be caring, competent and "in charge" without abusing their power and authority.

- Clear and direct communication is valued, practiced and taught.

- Student success is measured not only by academic achievement but also by the physical, mental, social and emotional health of students.

- Avoidance of stereotyping and bias while still acknowledging and valuing diversity.

- An attitude of "we are all in this together" rather than an "us vs. them" mentality, including a sense of partnership with parent/guardians and the community.

- Opportunities for students to get to know and work with students who are different from them.

- Refusal to allow sexual and other forms of harassment and bullying.

- Conflict resolution, problem-solving skills and violence prevention programs built into the curriculum.

- Policies and procedures are proactive and preventive in nature, including but not limited to crisis management planning and the creation of a safe school climate.

These qualities should exist across the entire school community. In positive school environments, the values and characteristics described above are present among the student population, among the staff, faculty and administration, and between the students and the adults in the school. Ideally, these qualities are also present at the school board level and in all interactions with parents/guardians and community members.

Skill 6.2   Effective Communication Skills

Effective communication is essential to the school counselor's ability to do her or his job successfully. The need to listen and respond well cannot be overestimated. Good communication is not only important in order to meet the needs of the students, but also to enhance the functioning of the guidance department and the school's capacity to respond to student needs.

Equally important, however, is the modeling that effective communication provides to students. Good role models are invaluable to students of all ages. When the school counselor shows students how to pay attention to others, express ideas and opinions, make suggestions, and ask questions clearly and respectfully, he or she is teaching skills that students can use throughout their lifetimes. In addition to modeling, the school counselor may find it helpful to actually offer programs that teach good communication skills in order to promote the student's social and personal development.

The essential elements to effective communication are these:

- Listening attentively without interrupting.

- Responding in ways that the speaker knows that she or he has been heard, including direct appreciation and validation of the speaker's views.

- Articulating ideas, opinions, observations and questions clearly and directly.

- Seeking clarification rather than making assumptions about what the other person is saying.

- Maintaining an attitude of respect at all times, including word usage, voice tone, facial expressions and other non-verbal behavior.

- Working to manage one's emotional reactions so they don't interfere with good communication (e.g., not taking others' comments personally).

Listening and Responding Skills

Listening is a highly subjective and selective activity. Listening is not just hearing words but grasping the meaning the speaker wishes to impart when those words are uttered. The meaning of the words spoken and interpreted depends upon the subjective world of both the speaker and the listener.

Some barriers to good listening are the following:

1. Hearing what you want to hear, not what is actually said.

2. Not hearing what is said at all due to one's own need to speak. Waiting for the other person to finish so we can speak causes us to think about what we are going to say instead of listening to what is being said.

3. We exhibit biased listening when we form an opinion about the value of what is being said and therefore discount the meaning of the words.

4. Emotions, either negative or positive can cause interference with our listening abilities.

5. The presence of both internal and external distractions.

Elements of Good Listening Skills

Effective listening not only involves tuning into the spoken words of the speaker but perceiving the tone of voice, the nonverbal cues given by the speaker and the emphasis given to the words. A good listener is one who consistently, under many circumstances, accurately understands the speaker's meaning by using their listening skills together with their thinking processes.

Lyman Steil developed the SIER Model which includes four stages of listening. These are *sensing*, the attending to a stimulus; *interpreting*, assigning meaning to incoming information; *evaluating* the message by forming a judgment about what is heard; and finally *responding* to the message.

Good listening skills include the following:

1. Create a positive atmosphere by being alert, attentive, and concentrating on the speaker.

2. Make eye contact and maintaining an expression of genuine interest.

3. Allow the speaker to finish a thought before responding.

4. Avoid critical judgments in your responses.

5. Make an effort to remember what has been said.

6. Avoid changing the subject unless there is a really good reason to do so. When you must change the subject, explain the reason for the change to the speaker.

7. Be as physically relaxed as possible, as such posture communicates that you have time to listen and are interested.

Elements of Good Responding Skills

There are a number of ways one can learn to respond to a speaker to let them know you have heard what he or she is trying to say. If you have listened well and thoughtfully to what the person is saying, your response will be appropriate, you will give good feedback and the speaker will feel good about the fact that you have heard what was said.

Good responding skills include:

1. Clarify the meaning of what was said by checking assumptions you have made as the listener to be sure you understand.

2. Continue to maintain eye contact as you give feedback.

3. Keep anger and other emotions out of the interaction. Try to express your feelings in a non-threatening way.

4. Help the other person in problem solving by responding positively and asking good questions.

5. Directly express your appreciation of the speaker's ideas, even if you disagree with them. You can address disagreements more effectively once you have thanked the speaker for sharing his/her ideas.

6. Be physically alert and use appropriate body language.

7. Reflect the person's feelings back to them.

8. Summarize the major ideas and concepts for further clarifications.

9. Use verbal and nonverbal reinforcers (such as head nods) to let the speaker know his/her message has been received.

10. Maintain a comfortable social distance.

11. Give constructive feedback: this is feedback that is descriptive not evaluative, offered not imposed, and focused on behavior rather than personal characteristics. Pay attention to the timing of feedback as well.

These websites offer useful tips on listening and responding skills: www.taft.cc.ca.us/lrc/class/assignments/actlisten.html, crs.uvm.edu/gopher/nerl/personal/comm/e.html, www.nasua.org/informationandreferral/TipSheet1ActiveListening.pdf , and www.psu.edu/dus/cfe/actvlstn.htm.

Skill 6.3   Interpersonal and Life Skills for Students

There are a range of interpersonal and life skills that the guidance department may help to teach students. The school counselor needs to have a good sense of the various methods of stress reduction, coping strategies, and problem-solving and time management approaches, as well as knowledge about diversity and nonviolence training (see Competency 16). Teaching interpersonal and life skills can occur on a one-to-one basis with students as the need arises, in a specialized small group format, or within classes such as health, psychology, consumer science, or sociology.

Problem-Solving, Stress Management and Coping Skills

Like communication skills, the capacity to cope effectively with challenges and the ability to manage stress well are important life skills. Learning such skills throughout the education process promotes students' social and personal development. Although some personality types are more naturally inclined to have positive coping skills, all students can learn new methods and improve their ability to solve problems and handle stress.

Some of the key ideas related to managing stress and coping with difficult situations have to do with attitude and approach. Being able to reframe a situation as a challenge rather than a threat is fundamental. This helps one to gain a measure of control over the challenge, and be able to see positive aspects in the situation, often reducing related anxiety and stress. Being able to think through a problem and develop possible outcomes is also important. Techniques such as biofeedback, meditation, exercise and relaxation are mind-body approaches that can mitigate stress. Time management and organizational skills are important coping and stress management skills as well.

Helping Students with Decision Making

The school counselor's role is to help students understand the decision making process, not make decisions for students. This need is particularly acute for adolescents who are facing many life choices. Supporting students actively as they approach decisions and teaching decision-making skills can help the student minimize the impact of any one decision causing irreversible harm to the student's present or future. An example of the need for good decision making skills is evident with regard to post-secondary education: a senior has received multiple offers from colleges and is uncertain about which offer to accept.

Elementary and middle school counselors may not face the same demands regarding student decision making. However, helping students with decisions regarding school projects, elective courses and extracurricular activities, for example, can facilitate better decision making at the high school level, and prepare students for employment and post-secondary education.

The process of decision making can be broken down into the following steps:

1. Define the problem clearly.
2. Formulate goals of ideal, acceptable and unacceptable outcomes.
2. Delineate all the possible options, including the option of making no decision at all.
3. Explore the barriers to all the options.
4. Explore the consequences of eliminating one or more of the options.
5. Narrow the options down to manageable choices.
6. Make an informed decision based upon the manageable choices.

Describing these steps to students as well as helping them with the practical application of these skills can be extremely helpful. Decision-making is best learned incrementally. Therefore, developmentally appropriate opportunities to make decisions at all educational levels results in adolescents who are more competent at making good choices.

Subarea: ASSESSMENT AND EVALUATION

COMPETENCY 7.0 Understand principles and characteristics of quantitative educational measurement, evaluation, and assessment methods

Skill 7.1 Major Tools and Functions of Appraisal

Assessment can take many forms and serve different purposes. The primary purpose of appraisal is to assist the counselor in helping students recognize their resources, utilize their strengths and accept their limitations, whether the focus is academic, social, personal or vocational. Increasingly, tests are used to measure student performance for reasons other than helping individual students with their educational and career goals. Nonetheless, it is the task of the counselor to assist the student in using all test results for self-understanding and growth.

Formal Assessment Tools

A variety of instruments are used for evaluation purposes. Formal tools with standardized scoring include tests administered by school counselors and other personnel as well as tests administered by the school psychologist. The school psychologist might utilize intelligence tests, which assess the ability to learn, as well as other psychological and aptitude tests in order to determine appropriate placement and develop individualized educational plans when needed.

School counselors, teachers and others may administer achievement tests (which evaluate how much has been learned), state tests measuring student performance, college entrance and preparatory tests (such as SAT, PSAT, and ACT), advanced placement (AP) tests, and others. These tests, while administered at school, are scored offsite by the testing company who prepares and distributes the tests.

Other formal means of appraisal include inventories that measure aptitude, vocational interests, personality traits, and learning styles. Many of these are scored by the school counselor or other personnel administering the test. Counselors may also use assessment tools designed to hone in on behavioral issues such as the incomplete sentence test, lethality inventories, suicide risk assessments, and depression inventories. These need to be used with caution and only with appropriate background and training.

Informal Assessment Tools

School counselors may find they use more informal means of assessment on a more frequent basis. These may involve using some of the inventories mentioned above as discussion tools rather than as formal assessments, behavioral observation of the student in the classroom or other settings, feedback forms developed to evaluate specialized guidance programs, behavior surveys, and needs assessments. The value of all informal assessment tools lies in their ability to give the counselor information that can enhance his or her work with students, and, in many cases, increase the student's self-awareness.

Appraisal can be used for these purposes:

1. To help students recognize and utilize the resources within themselves.

2. To improve self-understanding and to enhance self-concepts.

3. To assess the student's behavior and help the counselor and student anticipate the student's future behavior.

4. To stimulate the student to consider new interests for further exploration and to develop realistic expectations.

5. To provide meaningful information that can help the student make intelligent decisions.

6. To aid the counselor and student in identifying and developing future options.

Appraisal also has limitations. These include the following:

1. The use of tests can, at times, interfere with the relationship the counselor has developed with the student, especially if the student is sensitive to being evaluated.

2. There may be a tendency to allow test results to dictate a course of action without considering many other factors. Care needs to be taken not to make assumptions about the student's abilities and choices based on testing alone.

3. If the results of the test are not presented to the student in a manner that promotes self-understanding, more damage than good can result from taking the test.

4. The use of tests tends to put the counselor in the position of an authority, so the student may perceive the test results as the absolute truth.

5. Many informal assessment tools, while helpful in generating discussion, can be used subjectively by both the counselor and the student.

Assessment for Other Purposes

Ideally, tests are administered when the student feels the need for additional information for decision making regarding educational or career development planning. If the student makes the decision to take a test, motivation is high and this enhances the test's accuracy. Some tests are administered according to the school district's or the state's mandate. These are primarily performance and achievement tests. The stated purpose is to assess the effectiveness of the school's educational programs and identify areas needing improvement, based on student achievement levels.

Conditions Affecting Test Results

Testing Room Environment - The comfort of the room and the desk or table and chairs can affect the outcome of the test. The room should be well lighted and ventilated, free of noise and extraneous sound. A minimum distance should be maintained between desks, alternating seats if possible, and the students should be able to hear the directions clearly. The desk should be large enough to provide enough writing space for both the test and the answer sheet

Physical and Mental Condition of the Test Taker - The scores obtained on any test depend to a certain extend on the student's physical and mental condition. Tests should never be scheduled to conflict with other school activities. These would include, but are not limited to, exam week for termination of courses in progress, vacations, and extracurricular activities such as proms and sports events. Students tend to underestimate their physical stamina and do not take into consideration the fact that physical exhaustion impacts mental function.

Related conditions that are beyond the control of the counselor include the stress level of the student, the atmosphere at home, and social interactions students are having with peers that may have erupted immediately before the exam.

Preparation of the Test Taker- This includes both academic preparation (if an achievement test is to be administered) and the preparation given to the student about the mechanics of the test. Motivation to do well on the exam is also an important part of preparation.

Validity of the Test - If the test does not test what it is supposed to test, there is no reason to administer the exam. It is not only a waste of the student's and counselor's time, but it is detrimental to the motivation of the student in sitting for future tests. There is also the added danger of using incorrect and invalid results to determine future goals and placements.

Skill 7.2 Knowledge of Measurement Concepts

The language of testing is unique, and knowledge of interpretation of test data is an important part of the appraisal procedure. Some common terms used in testing and measurement are:

Correlation coefficient - a statistical concept in test validity that measures the relationship between two factors.

Derived score - any score that is not a raw score. It is obtained from a formula that uses the raw score data.

Norming - the scores obtained by a randomly selected group of test takers for the purpose of comparison to future groups of test takers to determine uniform levels of success on the tested information.

Raw Score - the basic score that is usually obtained by counting the number of answers right. It can also be obtained by using the number of answers wrong. The authors of the test can determine any other way to define a raw score. The way the score is defined is noted in the test manual.

Reliability - how dependable or consistent the test is. The three types of reliability are: 1) **scorer reliability:** how consistently different scorers arrive at the same score; often used as a measurement when grading essays or subjective tests; 2) **content reliability**: the degree to which all questions measure the content; 3) **temporal reliability**: how dependable the test is over a long period of time.

Reliability coefficient - a statistical concept in test validity that measures how reliable the relationship is between two factors.

Standard deviation - the specific interval between bands of scores; each interval indicates a different level of achievement.

Standard error of measurement - the inaccuracy of a test caused by chance. Every test has some element of inaccuracy or unreliability so this element of the test is taken into consideration when evaluating the test results. The degree of error is reported in the use of the term standard deviation, which is a band of scores. The formula is this: the square root of 1 minus the reliability coefficient, thus obtaining the standard error of measurement.

Standard score - an indication of the distance between the raw score and the mean of the norm in terms of the standard deviation.

Standardization - Researchers, other than the authors of the test, have provided the protocol to be used to administer the exam, including the provision that the test will be given and scored in the same way at each administration.

Stanine - an interpretation of placement often used in achievement tests. It is a measurement that runs from 1 to 9 and is a band of about one-half a standard deviation in width. Scores are based on percentile values.

Usability - the consideration given to cost, ease of administration, and time taken to score in the administration of the test.

Validity - This is the concept of "does the test, test what it is supposed to test?" In other words, how meaningful is the test? There are four types of validity:

1) **face validity**: Does it look like it may test what it should? (This is not a very dependable source of information.)

2) **content validity**: Is there a close connection between what is taught and what is being tested?

3) **construct validity**: What is the statistical relationship between the scores and another variable that should relate to the test?

4) **empirical validity**: What is the correlation coefficient between the scores and some standard of performance?

TEACHER CERTIFICATION STUDY GUIDE

COMPETENCY 8.0 Understand how to manage, administer, and interpret a variety of educational assessment programs and instruments

Skill 8.1 Procedures Involved in Appraisal Administration

In many cases, the test materials are sent to the school counselor (or other administrator) by the company who has devised and will be scoring the test. When the test materials are received by the administrator of the test, they should be counted and the amount compared to the number on the invoice in order to insure the accuracy of the number of tests received. If possible, they should be placed in a safe with a combination lock known only to a few trusted school personnel. If this is not possible they should be put under locked storage in an area of the school that is not accessible to students and non-authorized personnel.

A day or so before the test, the exams should be counted again to confirm that the tests have been kept secure. The tests should be divided according to the room setup and the number of students to be tested. They should then be replaced in the safe location and not taken out until shortly before the test is to be administered. At that time there should be a person in authority present with the tests at all times. Tests should never be left in a room without a proctor. When the students are given a test break, the tests should be closed and the room locked when the students leave.

After the exam is completed the following procedures should be adhered to:

A. Collecting

The proctor should count each exam and answer sheet as it is being collected. If the tests are numbered, each numbered test should be accounted for in order to insure two tests were not given out inadvertently. The students should not leave the room until all the exams and answer sheets are in order.

B. Storing

The tests should be placed in the safe location until it is time for scoring. If the tests are to be returned to the testing company for scoring they should be packaged immediately and prepared for mailing. The service selected for transportation should be notified and a pick-up date should be scheduled as soon as possible. In the meantime the packaged material should be placed in the safe location until picked up for transportation.

C. Safeguarding Data and Testing Instruments

As mentioned, the testing material should be kept confidential at all times until the counselor is released from the responsibility of protecting the tests or when it becomes the responsibility of other professionals. Access to the data results should be available only to authorized personnel. This includes the counselor, the parent/guardian, the student, and possibly a teacher or other school personnel or administrator.

If individuals outside the school community (such as the media or an attorney) want access to the information, permission must be obtained in writing from the student (or parent/guardian if the student is a minor). The information could also be released by a court order if necessary. Legally, the counselor has no authorization to give any information about a student without such permission.

Skill 8.2   Interpreting Assessment Data

Sharing Data with Other Professionals both Inside and Outside the School

The counselor must make every effort to safeguard the assessment results. School personnel should not have access to such data unless they are directly involved in providing services to the student, such as the school psychologist, special education teacher or school social worker. Generally, a need-to-know basis is the guideline. Under most circumstances, clerical staff, teachers and others should not have access.

While psychotherapists, social workers and other professionals outside the school who are involved with the student are bound by the ethics of confidentiality to which the school counselor is bound, this material cannot be released with the express written permission of the student and/or parent/guardian(s). Once a release is obtained, all material relating to the student sent to these people should contain whatever is necessary for the recipient to help the student.

Test scores can be reported directly, as well as the counselor's interpretation of these scores and observations of the student when the scores were presented. This interpretation requires knowledge of the test, its structure and intent, and the scoring guidelines even if the scoring was done offsite. Such information needs to be direct and focused, and should not contain speculation or opinion not based on data. It is particularly important for counselors to be cautious in sharing the results of informal assessment tools.

Interpreting Student Data from Written Reports

The counselor quite often is on the receiving end of written reports about students from various sources. These can be from a reading clinic, a psychiatrist or psychologist, a social worker or a teacher. It is important that the counselor is knowledgeable about the material in the report and, if some of the material is not understandable, investigate further for clarification. If the counselor is to counsel the student based upon these written reports, accuracy in interpretation is essential. Quite often it is appropriate for the counselor to seek a telephone or personal meeting with the writer in order to clarify and consult about the material in the report, as well as collaborate on an action or treatment plan. As with all confidential student information, written permission must be obtained prior to consulting with another professional outside the school district.

TEACHER CERTIFICATION STUDY GUIDE

COMPETENCY 9.0 Understand how to use assessment and evaluation information and data to plan educational programs and school improvement

Skill 9.1   Using Assessment Data

Assessment data can be used at the micro-level (for individual student educational planning) and at the macro-level (for overall school and curricular improvement). Some assessment tools yield information that is useful at both levels; other tools are designed to provide specific information for a specific purpose. Clarity about the intent of the tools and methodology to be employed is essential in gathering and utilizing accurate and informative assessment data.

When the goal of testing is for school improvement or program development, individual scores are generally less important than the aggregate data. In other words, individual performance is not the focus. Rather, the collective performance of students in a particular grade, class, curricular area or program is the goal and results should be reported as such. In these situations, the way in which the test results are reported and interpreted is generally dictated by the design of the test. However, school counselors, teachers and administrators may find that a detailed review of the test results can provide insight into avenues for school improvement not necessarily outlined by the general methodology.

Assessment Data Related to Individual Students

All test results for individual students should be recorded and retained for use at another time, for comparison purposes, or for meetings with parents and others working with the student. Therefore a written record or report should be created. Results must be converted into an understandable form and presented in a format that is understandable to the person receiving that report; whether it is one highly trained in interpretation, one moderately trained, or someone with no training at all. In all cases, dissemination of test results should be on a "need to know" basis and only with the required permission.

There are many ways a written report can be created. These include, but are not limited to, a narrative format delineating the past and present record of the student, a graph form such as horizontal or bar graphs, or as a profile chart. Ins some cases, recommendations for the application of the assessment data may be included. The language of testing should be incorporated in the written report to insure consistency in interpretation by all professionals using the data.

Skill 9.2   Reporting Assessment Results to Students and Parents

The role of the counselor is not only to supply information to the authorized people concerned with the results of tests, but to be certain the results are interpreted and understood as accurately as possible. The communication of the test results should involve interacting and responding to the feelings and concerns of the student and his/her parent/guardian(s). Test results can be threatening to students and parents. They often feel results are absolutes and reflect a rigid evaluation of the student. Sensitivity to the feelings and needs of the student and the parent are primary in communicating results.

Since counseling is a confidential relationship, the counselor should obtain permission from the student to reveal any information given in confidence. This may sometimes apply to test scores given to parent/guardian(s). At the least, notification to the student that the parent will be receiving the scores and a verbal approval should be obtained.

Once it is clear that the parents are to receive the test report, the counselor should work with the parent in a counseling relationship. Parent/guardian(s) may not react objectively to the child's test results. If they do not agree that the results are consistent with their concept of the child's ability, it may be difficult for them to accept the results. Nevertheless, parents have a right to know, and, to best help their child, need the opportunity to see realistically the abilities of their child. In communicating with the parents, the counselor must be empathetic about the difficulty of accepting new information, and recognize the understanding level of the parent and communicate at that level.

The following techniques of test interpretation are useful in communication.

1.   The interpretation should be related to the goals of the counseling.
All counselor-student relationships are based upon the needs of the student and his/her individuality. Therefore, sharing test data should be framed in this context. The student should be prepared and ready to receive the information and relate it, with the help of the counselor, to the predetermined goals of testing.

2. The results of the test belong to the student.
The goal of testing is to enhance the student's understanding of his/her interests, capabilities, and behavior. The student is entitled to the test results in a timely manner and there should not be a hesitation on the part of the counselor to withhold unfavorable results. Facing the reality of one's abilities is part of the maturation process. This cannot occur if the truth is not communicated or is colored in a manner that could be misinterpreted.

3. The perception of the student to the scores is of the utmost importance.
If the testing results conflict with self perception, the student could have emotional difficulties in accepting the information. This is where the skill and experience of the counselor comes into play. The goal of the counselor is to help the student and parents accept the information and build upon this new data. The counselor can enhance the likelihood of acceptance by striving to frame the all information (even seemingly negative results) as useful and instructive.

4. Provision should be made for individual interpretation.
It is preferable to interpret test results individually, but often the nature of the test and the number of individuals tested does not lend itself to individual counseling. When group interpretation is required, it is desirable to impress upon the students that individual consultation about their scores is available. In the group setting, the procedure is limited to explaining the purpose of the test and the norm group to which the students have been compared. Individual results should never be announced in the group. Statistics as to what scores are in different stanines or other ranges should be explained so students can evaluate their own results. The counselor should plan on conferring with individual students whose scores are low or whom the counselor knows will be concerned about their scores or when testing is the result of the counseling process.

5. The counselor must be thoroughly familiar with the test.
If the counselor does not understand the significance of the test results, accurate interpretation of the results cannot be expected. Therefore, it is imperative for accuracy as well as credibility purposes that the counselor is thoroughly familiar with the test that has been administered.

6. Interpretation sessions should be structured.
The purpose of structuring is to do away with the mystery of the testing situation, to help the student identify and correct mistaken impressions and to face some realities the results may reveal. Other issues of concern to the student and the parent/guardian(s) should be addressed at another interview, if possible.

7. Test results, not scores, should be communicated at a meaningful level to the student.
The purpose of reporting test results instead of scores is to help students use the information to form more realistic self-concepts. Scores in and of themselves do not impart information about the test taker. The student should understand the implications the results may have for the future. If the student does not understand the information presented, the most accurate information can be useless. Objectivity is the goal of the counselor in presenting the information, so counselor judgments and opinions should not be part of the process. It is also important the counselor explain the language used in the test results, the norming group to which the comparison is being made and the relationship between the score and the present and future goals of the student.

8. The student should help in the interpretation of the results.
This participation allows the counselor to see if the student understands the test results, encourages the student to contribute new information about him/herself into the counseling process, and tends to make the results more acceptable to the student.

9. Test results should, if possible, be verified by other information.
These data could consist of information from others who are familiar with the student as well as information from the students themselves.

10. The counselor, above all, must present the data and results honestly.
If the counselor suspects the student is disappointed with the results, the counselor must make an effort to support the student and explore the student's needs in light of the test results. Additional personal counseling sessions may be in order.

TEACHER CERTIFICATION STUDY GUIDE

Subarea: COUNSELING AND GROUP GUIDANCE

COMPETENCY 10.0 Understand principles and techniques of individual counseling

Skill 10.1 The Scope of the School Counselor's Role

The number of guidance activities that the counselor provides for students can be quite extensive, depending on the expectations of the school administrators, the specific job requirements in a particular school setting, and the interests and temperament of the counselor. Some guidance departments divide up tasks such as coordinating all testing, serving as liaison with military and college recruiters, or being the contact person for the local vocational high school. In other districts, school counselors may function in all areas of guidance, even in more than one school and/or level (i.e., elementary, middle or junior high, and high school).

The major tasks of the school counselor are to be a guide and advisor for students and a conduit of information on various topics. The counselor's role often constitutes a kind of "connective tissue" among students, teachers, parents/guardians, and the administration. This is loosely referred to as "counseling."

The school counselor's role may vary significantly from one school district to the next regarding the nature of personal, individual counseling. Some districts expect the school counselor to provide ongoing counseling in varied formats as well as crisis intervention and referral. Others limit the work of the counselor to very short term work, focused primarily on the identification of problems with subsequent referral to community resources. Each counselor needs clarity from the head of the department and the school administrators about the scope of his or her work.

With the exception of specialized schools or alternative education programs, most counselors in a school setting are not in a position to provide in-depth mental health counseling. The demands on counselors are many, and the school environment cannot provide the kind of intervention and support some students require. Effective short term counseling with referral for mental health evaluations by qualified personnel in the community often best meets the needs of students. Ongoing therapy should be provided by community agency clinicians or private practitioners in the area. Early identification of substance abuse and mental health concerns followed by collaboration with parent/guardian(s) and appropriate outside referrals can be key functions for school counselors.

Educational and career counseling generally fall within the purview of the school counselor's role. Other counseling tasks may involve short-term, target-specific psycho-educational groups such as anger management or interpersonal skill development, as well as crisis and/or grief counseling in the event of a death or other trauma in the school community.

Regardless of the extent of a counselor's work in counseling students, there is general agreement that school counselors should not be in the position of school disciplinarian. While there may be an occasion when the school counselor must "write up" a student for a disciplinary problem, as would any faculty or staff member, disciplinary matters should routinely be handled by someone outside of the guidance department. Counselors need to be able to earn and maintain the trust of students; if students don't feel safe with counselors, they are unlikely to seek help from them, or disclose sensitive information to them. Serving as a disciplinarian can undermine trust and interfere with counseling relationships.

Individual Counseling

In many school settings, short-term individual counseling is the most common form of intervention. This modality can be utilized spontaneously as problems arise. Further, it is not limited by the scheduling confines of group counseling. The counselor can tailor the interventions to the particular student's needs and make the most of each session. Drawing on varied techniques, the school counselor can respond to immediate situations as well as longer term issues in individual counseling, helping the student effect change in his or her life.

Sometimes, a school counselor may engage in short term (one to three sessions) counseling with a student, and then determine that the student needs a more intense level of intervention. At this point, a referral for therapy may be made to a community agency or private practitioner. The school counselor's role then shifts to one of follow-up and support. This role is important and should not be seen as less substantial but rather one of changed focus. The student may continue to rely on the counselor as a touchstone and source of information and reassurance, often allowing the outside therapy to be more productive than it might be otherwise.

Trust and Confidentiality

The ability to create rapport and meaningful relationships with students and others is the sign of an effective counselor. When the counselor has the trust of the student, the student is much more likely to listen to and act on the counselor's suggestions. Keeping information confidential, within the confines of the need for parental notification and other school policies, is essential to building trust.

If the counselor does not keep information confidential, trust is destroyed, and it is harder to help the student grow and mature. Trust is built up gradually. In order to facilitate trust, information given to the student must always be true, accurate and timely. The counselor must be a visible presence in the school, and be available to students. There are many ways to make contact with students, both formally and informally. When such an atmosphere of accessibility is created, students will be much more inclined to contact the counselor in time of need and crisis.

Skill 10.2 Major Counseling Theories and Approaches

In Skill 1.1 we addressed several major human development theories that also include counseling approaches and techniques. The theories detailed below are intended to augment the information in Skill 1.1

COGNITIVE-BEHAVIOR THERAPY

In cognitive-behavior therapy clients explore reasons for their behavior by understanding their thoughts. They are also encouraged to look at the ramifications of their behavior on themselves, others, and the environment in which they live and function.

One of the major approaches in the field of cognitive-behavior therapy is *Rational-Emotive Therapy*, **also referred to as Rational-Emotive Behavior Therapy (REBT). Albert Ellis** founded of Rational-Emotive Therapy and is effectively the grandfather of all cognitive-behavior therapies. He believed that the concepts of insight and awareness into childhood events did not result in the resolution of present emotional dysfunction. He also theorized that the connection between the past and the present was not explored fully in psychoanalytic theories.

The key concept in RET holds that even though emotional malfunction is rooted in childhood disturbances, individuals continue to reinforce their irrational and illogical thinking. Emotional problems are the result of irrational beliefs that need to be challenged in order for the individual to resolve the emotional reaction.

The **A-B-C** approach to personality is the basis of RET therapy: A=activating event, B=belief system, C=consequences. RET stresses action and practice in combating irrational and self-delusional ideas. The thinking and belief systems of the client are considered the basis for all personal problems. RET techniques include directed, time-limited, structured approaches for treating depression, anxiety, and phobic behavior. Further developments of cognitive-behavior theory are Aaron Beck's cognitive theory and Donald Meichenbaum's cognitive-behavior modification theory.

Donald Meichenbaum's cognitive-behavior theory has three phases. Clients are instructed to monitor their own behavior in order to identify negative thoughts and feelings. This is called the conceptual phase. The next phase is rehearsal, where the client creates a new internal system by substituting positive thoughts and feelings. In the application phase, the client applies more effective coping skills to real life situations. Focusing on the client's inner speech is a technique that is used in cognitive-behavior modification theory.

Similarly, **Aaron Beck** emphasized the assumption that clients' conversations with themselves play a major role in their behavior. He theorized that the way people feel and behave is based one the way they view their experiences. The therapy is short-term, active, focused and insightful. Beck's concept of automatic thoughts is the idea that certain events trigger emotional responses. The goal of therapy is for clients to recognize and discard self-defeating thinking and correct erroneous beliefs. It has been applied particularly to the treatment of depression. The techniques used in all cognitive-behavioral therapies are derivative of the above theorists and are tailored to the needs of the client. Any method that works may be used, though there is a bias towards approaches with empirical validation.

Cognitive techniques include disputing irrational beliefs, homework, humor and the changing of language to a more positive approach. *Emotive techniques* include imagery, role-playing and shame attacking procedures. *Behavioral techniques* include operant conditioning, self management and modeling. RET is directive, persuasive and confrontational in contrast to cognitive therapy which emphasizes dialogue to discover misconceptions.

Contributions of *cognitive-behavioral* therapy are:

1. Counseling tends to be brief and outcome-focused.

2. Practice and experimenting with new behaviors is emphasized.

3. The therapy stresses the clients' ability to control his/her experience of the world.

4. It is easily used with clients who are action-oriented and willing to accept responsibility for their difficulties.

5. The therapy can be effectively employed in crisis situations.

Limitations of *cognitive-behavioral* therapy are:

1. The underlying reasons for irrational beliefs is not explored, leaving the client open to incorporate additional different irrational beliefs into their belief system.
2. The dialogue aspect of the therapy does not lend itself to working with clients of low intelligence.
3. There is the danger of the therapist imposing his/her views on the client with the potential for psychological harm.
4. Emotional issues are not explored which may limit the effectiveness of the therapy in the long run.

Some of the key terms of *cognitive-behavioral* theory and therapy are:

A-B-C Model - the construct stating that one's problems do not originate from events but from the beliefs one holds about those events. Changing one's beliefs is the best way to change negative feelings.

Arbitrary Inferences - the distorted view of making conclusions without the basis of supporting and relevant evidence; part of Aaron Beck's cognitive therapy.

Automatic Thoughts - ideas (usually outside one's awareness) triggered by a particular event that lead to emotional reactions.

Cognitive Errors - misconceptions and wrong assumptions on the part of the client.

Cognitive Homework - the process used to help a client learn to deal with anxiety and to challenge irrational thinking.

Cognitive Restructuring - the process of replacing negative thoughts with positive thoughts and beliefs.

Cognitive Therapy - a type of therapy focused on changing negative behavior by changing false thinking and beliefs.

Collaborative Empiricism - a concept from Aaron Beck's cognitive therapy that views the client as capable of making objective interpretations of his/her behavior, along with the collaboration of the therapist.

Coping Skills Program - a set of procedures to help clients deal with stressful situations by changing their thinking.

Disputational Method - a method taught to clients in RET to help them challenge irrational beliefs.

Distortion of Reality - inaccurate thinking causing one to act irrationally, emotionally, and subjectively.

Internal Dialogue/Inner Speech - the process used to recognize irrational thoughts.

Irrational Belief - an unreasonable thought leading to emotional problems.

Labeling and Mislabeling - the distorted view of basing one's identity on imperfections and mistakes made in the past.

Musturbation - the word used by Albert Ellis to describe beliefs grounded in *musts, shoulds, and oughts;* a rigid and absolute way of thinking.

Overgeneralization - the distorted process of forming rigid beliefs based upon a single event and then applying them to subsequent events.

Personalization - the tendency for individuals to relate events to themselves when there is no basis for this connection.

Polarized Thinking - a cognitive error of based on an all-or-nothing framework. There are no gray areas in polarized thinking.

Rationality - a way of thinking that will help us attain our goals.

Role-playing - the process of helping a client work through irrational beliefs by practicing new behaviors.

Selective Abstraction - the distorted view of forming conclusions based on an isolated detail of an event.

Self-Instructional Therapy - the concept that the self-talk an individual indulges in directly relates to the things they do in every day life. The therapy consists of training the client to modify self-talk, a form of cognitive restructuring or cognitive behavior modification developed by Donald Meichenbaum.

Shame-Attacking Exercises - a technique of RET encouraging the individual to do things about which they feel shame without believing they are foolish or without becoming embarrassed

Stress-Inoculation Training - a cognitive-behavior modification technique aimed at giving the client the coping tools to restructure the thoughts that lead to stress, and to rehearse the behavior changes in order to solve the emotional problems caused by stressful situations.

EXISTENTIAL THERAPY

The evolution of existential therapy developed as a reaction to the theories of psychoanalysis and behaviorism. Existential theory differs from the psychodynamic and behavior theories in their fundamental presumptions about the nature of human beings. Psychodynamic theories are based upon a deterministic view of human nature; they see personal freedom controlled by irrational actions, past occurrences, and the unconscious. The behaviorists believe freedom is restricted by societal forces.

Existentialists believe the early theorists did not take into account all aspects of human nature. By concentrating on external objective factors, the psychodynamic theorists and the behaviorists ignored the internal frame of reference and subjective experiences of the individual. Existentialists concern themselves with questions of freedom, responsibility and choice, and the meaning of reaching one's full potential. This philosophical basis suggests people must create their own meaning through their choices in a world that is fundamentally meaningless and lonely; the individual must explore what it means to be fully human.

The assumption is that we are free and therefore responsible for our actions and the results of those actions and choices. We are the "authors of our lives" and are not the victims of circumstances because we have the freedom to change those circumstances. See www.existentialpsychotherapy.net for more information.

Some of the early European existentialists were **Ludwig Binswanger**, **Karl Jaspers**, **Medard Boss** and **Viktor Frankl**. Contemporary figures are **Rollo May** and **Irvin Yalom**. Their work is based upon the work of philosophers Dostoyevsky, Heidegger, Nietzsche, Sartre and Buber.

Viktor Frankl expounded the theory of logotherapy, which literally means "healing through reason" (logic). In developing this approach, Frankl was influenced by the earlier European existentialists. Logotherapy is designed to help people find meaning in life through their experiences.

Irvin Yalom wrote Existential Psychotherapy, a central text in the field of existential psychotherapy. In it, he addresses the core issues that make up the existential theory: isolation, meaninglessness, freedom and death within the context of the therapeutic relationship and process.

Rollo May is responsible for converting the European philosophy of existentialism into American theory and practice. He focuses on the subjective aspects of the therapy and believes that freedom and responsibility go hand in hand, with freedom requiring us to accept responsibility for who we become.

This theory requires an intellectual and philosophical approach on the part of the therapist. Existentialist-based therapy is relationship-oriented, experiential and philosophical. It does not have a set regime of techniques but allows for incorporation of techniques from other therapies. The general approach is to focus upon four major concerns of human existence: freedom, isolation, death and meaninglessness.

The basic goals of existentialist therapy are to help clients become aware they are free to make choices to improve their experience of daily life. Clients are encouraged to see past and future choices, to accept the responsibility of their choices, to recognize the factors that hinder their freedom to choose, and to experience an authentic existence.

There are six concepts to which existential therapists ascribe. They are:

1. **We are capable of self-awareness**. The expansion of this awareness, a basic goal of the therapy, is to increase our perception of the freedom to choose and to act on those choices.

2. **We are free beings and must accept the responsibility of that freedom** to decide our own fate. Although we did not choose to be in this world, how we live here and what we do with our lives are our own choices. Each choice we make creates who we are. Whatever the set of circumstances, it is our attitude that determines how we approach a situation and how we survive it.

3. **In preserving our uniqueness, we know who we are** by our relations and interactions with others. Our awareness of this individuality makes us better able to lead an authentic life style.

4. **The meaning of our lives and existence are always in a state of fluidity** as we continue to create ourselves through our actions. These actions are the result of our own choices and we are not victims of forces beyond our control.

5. **Anxiety is a normal state**. It is part of the human condition, an emotional recognition of one's vulnerability and the responsibility of choosing in an uncertain world without any guarantees. Anxiety is the result of a person's awareness of their aloneness. It is not a sick condition, but rather a growth enhancer to motivate us to change conditions that have become intolerable.

6. **Awareness of death** is a human condition that gives meaning to living. Being aware of our ultimate death is the impetus for us to live our lives to the fullest. Life has meaning because it is not forever. The question is not how long we live, as we all will eventually die, but how we live that life, which creates meaning for our every day existence.

The focus of *existential* therapy is:

1. To confront the reality of being in the world alone and facing the anxiety of this isolation,

2. To understand one's subjective world,

3. To revise the assumptions arising from one's subjectivity, and

4. To make choices that lead to the living of an authentic life.

The approach is not based on curing sickness or solving immediate problems, but on utilizing the inherent knowledge of life experiences to live a fuller and more authentic existence.

Contributions of *existential* theory are:

1. The client-therapist relationship is based upon the humanity of the individual.

2. The theory addresses the major concerns of healthy individuals as they go through life cycles by concentrating on issues important to attaining life satisfaction.

3. The model allows for the inclusion of many other modalities within the larger philosophical framework provided by existential theory. In other words, psychodynamic explorations and cognitive-behavior techniques may be employed as part of the therapy.

The limitations of *existential* theory are:

1. A lack of a systematic procedure

2. The concepts can be difficult to comprehend, and require a particular orientation and effort on the part of the therapist.

3. There is no scientific research done on the model.

4. Lower functioning clients, clients in crisis who need immediate direction, and nonverbal clients may not be able to benefit from a philosophical and intellectual approach to problem solving.

Some of the key terms of *existential* therapy are:

Aloneness - a natural human condition from which we can derive strength to become free. When mastered we will have the ability to stand beside others to lend them support in their own aloneness.

Anxiety - the experience we have when we realize we are not immortal, that we face constant choices in an uncertain world, and when we realize we are fundamentally alone.

Authenticity - the ability to be true to our own ideas of a meaningful existence and to accept responsibility for the conditions of our lives, a result of the choices we have made.

Authorship - the concept that we create our own life situations, problems and destinies.

Awareness - the freedom to choose and act on our choices.

"Bad Faith" - the inauthenticity of not accepting the freedom to take responsibility for our own actions.

Existential Guilt - the result of the feelings we have when we permit others to shape our lives and make our choices.

Existential Neurosis - feelings of despair resulting from a failure to make our own choices.

Existential Vacuum - a condition of emptiness and depression that results from a meaningless lifestyle.

Existentialism - a philosophical movement that stresses individual responsibility for creating one's own ways of behaving, thinking, and feeling.

Freedom - the ability to be responsible for our own destiny and to be accountable for our own actions.

Logotherapy - a branch of existential therapy that challenges clients to search for meaning in life; developed by Viktor Frankl.

Meaninglessness - the fact that there is no inherent meaning in living, and it is up to us to create our own system of meaning.

Phenomenology - a method used in therapy to utilize subjective experiences as a therapeutic focus that is used in many existing theories.

Restricted Existence - the condition of one's functioning with a limited awareness of self and the inability to define the true nature of the problem.

"The Courage to Be" - our ability to live to our fullest, rather than living in within the constraints of what others expect; also, the ability to accept limitations and confront the feelings of emptiness that comes when we are to make new choices.

PERSON - CENTERED THERAPY

The founder of person-centered therapy was **Carl Rogers**. In the early 1940's Rogers created the "nondirective counseling" approach. Later he was involved in advocating for the encounter group movement and was a pioneer in the humanistic approach to counseling. He was opposed to the therapist acting as the expert whose advice dictated what the client needed to do to be well. He felt clients contain the ability to become a more fully functioning "self-actualized" person. Rogers believed all people have a "formative tendency" or inner energy which propels us towards fulfillment and self-actualization.

This theory rests upon the assumption that individuals have internal resources to work toward wholeness and self-actualization if properly supported and encouraged. Person-centered therapists believe clients can move forward constructively on their own. The focus is on understanding the feelings and thoughts expressed by the client from the vantage point of the client's subjective world. The theory emphasizes the personality and attitude of the therapist/facilitator, rather than concentrating on techniques (although the skills of active listening and reflecting are most often used).

This approach is a "way of being rather than a way of doing." Positive attitudes and behaviors on the part of the therapist create a climate of growth that not only reaches the client but which surrounds the client. This helps create an aura of "personal power," or the awareness of one's own feelings, needs and values, that is subsequently sensed by others and facilitates effective functioning.

The therapist's role is to create an atmosphere of empathy, acceptance, warmth and caring an environment of unconditional positive regard. The success of the therapy depends upon the therapist maintaining this climate as the major tool for facilitating positive outcomes for the therapy. In this environment, the client begins to drop defensive attitudes and concentrates more on meaningful goals, leading to positive and appropriate actions. Eventually the client uses the learning acquired in the safe environment of the therapy to apply to relationships outside the therapeutic setting. The focus is on experiencing and perceiving the immediate moment as an opportunity for change

Three characteristics of the therapist lend themselves to creating the atmosphere needed for client self-actualization:

Genuineness - the goal of person-centered therapists is to be aware of their feelings and attitudes, their shortcomings and their humility. They do not hide behind a professional demeanor, but align themselves with the person being counseled.

Unconditional Positive Regard - a positive, nonjudgmental acceptance and caring attitude on the part of the therapist.

Empathic Understanding - the ability to accurately sense the feelings and meanings of the client and to express these feeling and meanings so the client understands the therapist is truly in attuned to the client.

For more information about this approach, literature and training options, contact the Association for the Development of the Person Centered Approach at www.adpca.org.

The contributions of *person-centered* therapy are these:

1. The relevance of the therapist as a person breaks from more traditional forms of therapy and offers a more accessible model for some clients.

2. It is a relationship-centered therapy instead of a technique-centered therapy.

3. While the therapist assumes responsibility for creating an environment that is conducive to the client's success the responsibility for the direction of the therapy lies with the client.

4. The theory concentrates on a person's need to account for his/her inner experiences and has relied upon research to validate the concepts, practices and approach.

5. This theory inherently respects individual differences and therefore is very amenable to culturally competent therapy.

The major limitation of this approach is dependent upon the personal limitations of the therapists themselves. Limitations may include the following:

1. There can be lack of genuine empathy. The therapist may hold stereotypes about certain clients that make it difficult for a therapist to have positive regard, warmth, and acceptance for them.

2. The inability of the therapist to practice appropriate self-disclosure can be a problem. A person-centered approach requires that the therapist have the capacity to self-disclose, but also maintain boundaries. Finding this balance and being truly genuine requires a high degree of self-awareness and self-control on the part of the therapist.

3. Temperamentally, a therapist may not be best suited to the person-centered approach. The therapist may not listen well, or too readily makes assumptions. Further, the therapist may be anxious to solve problems rather than understand the problem to be solved, and have the capacity to allow the process of change to unfold.

4. The therapist may lack the belief that the client can change behavior, thus creating an atmosphere conducive to failure.

5. Person-centered therapy is not effective with people in crises situations who are looking for immediate problem solving strategies.

Some of the key terms of *person-centered* therapy are:

Accurate Empathic Understanding - the therapist's ability to sense the client's inner world (i.e., the client's subjective experience).

Congruence - a state in which self-experiences are accurately represented by self-concept; there is a matching of inner experience with external expressions; also refers to the genuineness of the therapist.

Facilitator - the role the therapist takes in person-centered therapy.

Genuineness - a state of authenticity resulting from self-analysis and a willingness to accept the truth of who one is.

Humanistic Psychology - a movement emphasizing freedom, choice, values, growth, self-actualization, spontaneity, creativity, play, humor and psychological health.

Nondirective Counseling - the type of counseling that assumes the client is the one who knows what is best and should not be in a passive role. This results in the therapist permitting the client to lead the counseling instead of the therapist doing the leading.

Incongruence - the discrepancy between self-concept and ideal self-concept. Incongruence usually results in anxiety, which can serve as a clue to the existence of a problem.

Internal Source of Evaluation - the process of looking to oneself for answers to problems.

Personal Power - the sense of strength that comes from knowing oneself and one's ability to mobilize energy. The therapist's ability to access his/her own personal power facilitates the client's development of personal power, rather than for controlling other people.

Self-Actualization - an inner growth force leading to the development of one's potential and the basis of people being trusted to resolve their own problems in a therapeutic relationship.

Therapeutic Conditions - the necessary conditions of the therapeutic relationship that allow the client to change. These conditions include therapist congruence, unconditional positive regard and accurate empathic understanding.

Unconditional Positive Regard - the acceptance of the client's right to all their feelings without conditions imposed by the therapist.

GESTALT THERAPY

Frederick Perls is considered the founder of Gestalt therapy. **Erving** and **Miriam Polster** were key figures in the development of Perls' concepts. The theory stresses the "here and now" and focuses upon bringing together the parts of the personality that are not integrated into the whole person. It also focuses on the "what and how" of behavior as well as the role unfinished business from the past plays in preventing the individual from adequately functioning in the present. The most frequent cause of unfinished business is resentment. Other sources of unfinished business are avoidance, guilt, anger grief and other feelings that remain unresolved.

Perls' theory includes the following five layers of neurosis:

1. The phony layer: acting as others wish us to act, playing games.
2. The phobic layer: avoiding the confrontation of who we really are.
3. The impasse layer: the sense of deadness or foreboding doom.
4. The implosive layer: fully experiencing our deadness.
5. The explosive layer: the releasing of phony roles to experience a feeling of relief.

Gestalt therapy is, in part, derived from existentialist therapy. Some of the major concepts of the therapy are:

- accepting responsibility for being in the here-and-now
- becoming aware of the present moment (itself a therapeutic process)
- facing the issues of avoidance
- dealing with impasses
- dealing with unfinished business from the past

Clients are expected to be active in their own therapy, to do their own interpreting, and to grow through personal contact. Gestalt therapists emphasize the awareness of personal contact at our boundaries with the world via our senses. This awareness is necessary for growth and change. The client resists contact by a variety of methods such as introjection, projection and retroflection. The goals of the therapy are:

- To challenge the client to develop methods of self-support in order to replace the environmental support system presently in effect
- To become more aware of the "here and now" and the self
- To recognize the parts of the self that have been denied
- To assume ownership and responsibility for this denial.

The focus is not on the techniques of the therapy, but on the therapist as a person and the role of helping the client make his/her own interpretations. The techniques of the therapy are to intensify direct experience in the moment. . Clients role-play and experiment with different scenarios to gain greater awareness of their inner conflicts and to intensify their experiences. In the role-playing aspects of the therapy, the therapist asks the client to play out all the roles experienced in a dream sequence, for example, in order for the client to better understand the dream. An "empty chair" may be placed in front of the client as a device to facilitate the expression of feelings.

More information about Gestalt theory and therapy, including access to key journals in the field, is available www.gestalt.org.

Some of the contributions of *Gestalt* theory are:

1. This approach can de-emphasize the intellectualization of the client's problems and focus on here-and-now experience of interpersonal contact.

2. It lends itself to brief therapy due to the intensity of the experiences of the client.

3. It utilizes dreams and unfinished business from the past in order to understand current problems.

4. The theory can be applied to group counseling, school and classroom problems, and workshop settings as well as individual counseling sessions.

Some limitations of *Gestalt* theory are:

1. It does not give much credence to cognitive factors, nor does it emphasize the importance of empathy and positive regard for the client.

2. It can become a technique-oriented theory with the potential of the therapist misdirecting the course of the therapy for the sake of the techniques.

3. The therapist can slip into autocracy, assuming the role of director rather than facilitator.

4. There is a lack of empirical research to validate the theory.

Some key terms in *Gestalt* therapy are:

Aboutism - the speaking of an incident in the past in contrast to speaking of the same incident in the present.

Avoidance - a technique used by clients to keep from facing unfinished business, from feeling uncomfortable emotions and from having to make changes in their life.

Awareness - the process of exploring one's thinking, feelings and actions.

Blaming Games - a technique used by the client to avoid taking responsibility for his/her growth, to avoid staying in the "now", and to prevent themselves from the pain of experiencing the "here and now".

Boundary Disturbance/Resistance to Contact - a technique practiced by individuals who attempt to control their environment; it can have both negative and positive consequences.

Confluence - the blurring of awareness of the difference between oneself and the environment.

Confrontation - the act of becoming aware of differences between verbal and nonverbal expressions, feelings and actions, and thoughts and actions.

Contact boundary – the interface or point of contact between an individual and the world around him or her, including other people.

Deflection - the process of distraction or inattention, making it difficult to sustain contact.

Dichotomy/Polarity - a split in which a person experiences opposing forces.

Explosive Layer - the mode of releasing the pretenses of phony roles in order to achieve a sense of relief and release.

Here-and-Now Awareness - the ability of the client to realize what s/he is experiencing in the present moment.

Impasse - the point at which we are stuck in a stage of less than full maturation. This may be accompanied by feelings of deadness or impending doom and a wish to avoid threatening feelings.

Implosive Level - the mode in which we allow ourselves to fully experience our deadness or inauthenticity. This leads to the chance to make contact with our genuine self.

Introjection - the acceptance of others' beliefs and standards without analyzing, assimilating and internalizing them.

Modes of Defense - the five layers of neurotic avoidance: the phony, the phobic, the impasse, the implosive and the explosive.

Phobic Layer - the mode of the avoiding of the emotional pain that comes with recognizing our real selves.

Phony Layer - the mode of reacting to others in stereotypical and inauthentic ways, in other words, playing games.

"Play the Projection" - a technique used to help clients see how they project onto others things they do not want to recognize in themselves.

Projection - disowning parts of ourselves by blaming them on the environment.

Resistance - defenses developed which prevent fully experiencing the present.

Retroflection - turning back to ourselves what we would like to do or have done to others.

Unfinished Business - unexpressed feelings (such as resentment, guilt, anger and grief) from childhood that are presently preventing effective psychological functioning; needless emotional garbage.

REALITY THERAPY

William Glasser developed the concept of reality therapy in the 1950s and 1960s. Originally, the approach emphasized individual responsibility. In the 1980s Glasser expanded this concept to a theory of control. Control theory emphasizes doing and thinking. The theory attempts to explain why and how people behave from the point of view of the subjective internal perception of their world. Glasser posits that the purpose of behaving the way we do is to eliminate the discrepancy between what we presently have and what we want.

The theory is also based upon the assertion that we are in charge of our lives, we choose our forms of behavior, and that behavior is intended to increase self-esteem and a sense of belonging, and to attain power and freedom. The therapy focuses on exploring ways to effectively manage our world so we can get what we want without hurting others in the process.

Reality therapy does not dwell on the past, the unconscious, the role of insight, or take into consideration the process of transference. Its goal is to help client clients acquire skills to take control of their lives, better cope with life's demands, and solve present day problems. The purpose is to achieve a satisfying, effective existence. The challenge in therapy is to examine how people are presently functioning in order to improve that functioning. The therapy is short-term and designed to help people develop a "success identity" by meeting the four psychological needs of belonging, power, freedom, and fun.
The therapist's relationship with the client is one of concern, support, and warmth. While the therapist is involved with clients in a positive way, he/she does not accept excuses for inappropriate behavior, and continuously prods and pushes to help the client accept reality and responsibility for his/her actions. The client is expected to take responsibility for deciding what goals to pursue and commit to those goals, to make value judgments about his/her current behavior, to plan a specific course of action for future success, and to make a commitment to carry out these plans in every day life.

The *WDEP model* is the procedure applied in the practice of reality-therapy.

W=Wants - Through questioning by the therapist, clients are able to express their wants, needs and perceptions of what is happening in every day life.

D=Doing - The therapist explores what clients are doing and what direction they are taking in their behavior to obtain those wants and needs.

E=Evaluation - The therapist encourages clients to evaluate their behavior patterns that help or do not help obtain those needs and wants.

P=Planning and Commitment - The therapist invites and encourages clients to plan for behavior change and commit to that change.

Glasser originally used his therapy in working with youthful offenders but the theory of control has been successfully used in individual, marital, family and group counseling, in alcohol and drug abuse clinics, and with students, teachers and administrators.

Contributions of *reality* theory are:

1. Clients are responsible for evaluating and changing their behavior.

2. The client is the catalyst in making specific plans, forming contracts for action and evaluating the success of these actions.

3. The emphasis is upon accountability. No excuses for failure are accepted but blame and punishment for not carrying out the stated changes are avoided. The focus instead is on what prevented the client from carrying out the plan of action and the readjustment to a more reasonable plan of action.

4. There is a structure to evaluate the degree and nature of the changes affected.

5. It is a short-term, clear and easily understood therapy that is applicable to different situations and clients, some of whom may not usually be receptive to other therapy approaches.

Limitations of *reality* therapy are:

1. Consideration is not given to feelings, the unconscious, and the past.

2. The influence of the culture and environment of the client is not taken into consideration when looking for alternatives to the maladjusted behavior. The focus is on the symptoms. The origin of the behavior is not taken into account.

3. There is a lack of research on reality therapy to establish its effectiveness.

Key terms of this approach are:

Autonomy - the acceptance of responsibility and the taking control of the direction of one's life; a state of maturity

Commitment - the ability on the part of the client to continue with a reasonable plan to effect the desired change

Control Theory - a theory of why people act the way they do; the internal motivation to master one's own world.

Involvement - the role of the therapist with the client in reality therapy, a vital part of establishing a relationship with the client.

Paining Behaviors - the manifestation of pain symptoms, such as depression, to refocus the problem on the symptoms instead of the behavior.

Perceived World - one's subjective world.

Picture Album - the perceived reality of the client formulated to meet their psychological needs.

Positive Addiction - the acts performed to gain psychological strength such as physical activity and meditation.

Responsibility - the dependable manner in which we satisfy our needs without interfering with the rights of others.

Success Identity - the state of self-esteem needed to fulfill the behaviors deemed necessary for attaining a more satisfying life experience. The end result of attaining a success identity is that the individual is able to give and receive love, has a sense of self-worth, and possesses the strength to create a satisfying life.

Total Behavior - the blend of the sum of all our activities that forms our personality and the person we have become.

Value Judgment - the evaluation of current behaviors to determine their value.

WDEP System - the abbreviation for the components of reality therapy: the identification of **w**ants, the **d**irection of behavior, the **e**valuation of self, and the **p**lan for change.

SOLUTION-FOCUSED THERAPY

Solution-focused therapy was initially developed by **deShazer** and **Berg** in recent years. The theory is based on work by various family therapists and the work of **Milton Erickson.** It is considered a brief therapy model, sometimes only comprising one session, which lends itself well to many guidance situations.

This model asserts that when clients come to counseling they have a picture of what they would like to be different about their lives and often have the answers to their problems. By providing a constructivist process, the counselor facilitates the process by helping the client in defining the problem, identifying viable solutions, and planning for working towards the desired behavior or reality. The core of solution-focused therapy lies not in the "why" but the "how." Theorists of this orientation argue that the past cannot be changed, so why not focus on how the client wants the future to be more satisfying?

Walter & Peller identified the following guides to making therapeutic choices:

1. Don't bother with what works. Make a determination to do more of it. Success can only be maximized.

2. Build on the small successes.

3. Experimentation is encouraged. Just because something has not been solved in the past it does not mean what was tried is the only possible solution.

4. Change is about the "here and now." Make the most of the current session.

A major focus of the work involves the counselor asking a range of questions to help draw out possible solutions. The solution-focused counselor first asks about the goal the client is hoping to achieve and is not dissuaded or discouraged it the client replies, "I don't know." The counselor empathically reframes these initial questions in order to solicit a goal. Effective goal-setting is critical to the success of solution-focused therapy.

The counselor facilitates the client's desire for change by asking what would be different if, after a night of sleep, the undesired behavior or situation had changed. The client is then engaged in a creative process of constructing a vision of positive behavioral difference or success. The counselor uses the vision as a framework upon which a solution will be defined.

Other questions are used to help the client identify desirable outcomes. The counselor's job is to reflect back the answers in ways that help clients better understand their strengths and skills as well as the nature of the problem. By the end of the session, the counselor assigns the solution as homework to practice in the time between the current and next session. The success of the applied solution can be reviewed in a following session, if there is one.

Contributions of *solution-focused* therapy:

1. Therapeutic work is accomplished with relatively few sessions.

2. Counseling is focused on the reality of the client and is not dependent on the interpretation of the client about past experience.

3. Clients are empowered to make change by what they envision of themselves through magical thinking.

4. The work is solution-focused, not problem-focused.

Limitations of *solution-focused* therapy:

1. Long-term and personality-based issues cannot be resolved by finding a solution.

2. Problems are over-generalized and oversimplified without in-depth consideration to the level of impact on the client's reality.

3. More empirical research needs to be conducted.

Some key terms of *solution-focused* therapy:

Coping questions - a series of questions the counselor uses to help the client identify previously unrecognized coping skills and strengths.

Exception-seeking question – a way to help clients discover the times when the identified problem does NOT trouble them.

Miracle question - a technique wherein the counselor encourages the client to imagine what it would be like if the problem he/she is facing were suddenly gone.
Scaling questions - a tool where clients rate the problem in varying degrees of severity in order to set goals and facilitate change.

Skill 10.3 Application of Counseling Theories and Techniques to a Specific Situation

Although there are a number of students who need counseling for emotional issues and/or have serious issues in their personal life, these problems usually come to the attention of school personnel when the child runs into trouble academically or displays disruptive classroom behavior. Once a student meets with the counselor, problems of a personal nature may be revealed. Addressing these problems within the context of the goal of success in school is part of the counselor's role.

TEACHER CERTIFICATION STUDY GUIDE

In the following case study, a student has been referred to the counselor because of poor performance. We will see what happens in the counseling situation to better understand what is going on with the student and how resolution was achieved.

In October Donna, a fifteen year old ninth grader, was referred to the school counselor because she was failing her first year algebra course. The teacher did not feel she was capable of doing the work and was suggesting that she drop the course and go into a general math class instead. This would fulfill her math requirement for high school graduation and she would not be behind one year in math. Donna objected to the move. Her parents wanted her to go to college and general math did not meet the requirements for college entrance. Donna had done well in middle school earning grades of 80's and 85's in eighth grade math. Her test scores on diagnostic math tests in May of the previous year when she was in eighth grade, indicated she performed at a 9.3 grade level.

Donna's mother was contacted by telephone and told of the teacher's concern. The mother felt Donna could do the work, that she was lazy and did not apply herself. In discussing with Donna her feelings about why she was failing, the counselor found Donna did not complete her homework assignments because she said when she ran into problems she had no way of solving them. When told she could come in after school for additional help from the teacher Donna said that the days the teacher had designated for extra help were days she had soccer practice.

In discussing a plan for Donna to be successful on the next unit exam in three weeks, it emerged that Donna participated in many non- school activities. She took dance lessons, was out of the house two nights a week for church meetings and to volunteer at the local nursing home reading to elderly patients. She had soccer games on the weekends and her family visited an ailing grandparent on Sundays. Donna had an older sister in her freshman year in college at a school out of town. Her father owned his own business and was active in local politics, and her mother was a teacher.

It was obvious to the counselor that Donna was juggling too many activities and did not have a block of time to devote to her studies. Although she was not failing any of her other courses, her grades were not high enough for entrance into the college that her sister attended and which her parents wanted her to attend. The problem as the counselor saw it was that Donna not only wanted to please her parents by participating in all the out of school activities, but her self esteem and self confidence were derived from these activities. She enjoyed them and did not want to give them up. She continued to think that she could pass the course simply by passing the final exam in June, a school policy.

GUIDANCE COUNSELOR

The counselor decided to use reality therapy with Donna. Donna had a study hall one period a day. She and the counselor decided to use this time for counseling and the teaching of study techniques in the counselor's office. Donna liked this idea as she realized she was not getting any studying done in the study hall because of the disruptive behavior of some of the other students. It was decided Donna and the counselor would talk for twenty minutes and Donna would do her math work for another twenty minutes. Since Donna did not have the time to see the teacher after school, a student from the honor society would come into the guidance office for twenty minutes every other day to help her study her math. Donna was pleased with this arrangement as the immediate problem of math was being addressed.

In the twenty minutes of counseling time the counselor focused on Donna's lifestyle. Donna had a need to keep busy every minute, the inability to say "no" to many of the projects her parents suggested she do after school, and she had feelings of guilt for her own need to sometimes just do nothing. It was difficult for Donna to accept the fact that she was not able to juggle all these activities, and do well in all of them. She also struggled with the reality that she needed to be able to prioritize and think through what she felt was important in her life, rather than relying on her parents to make these decisions for her. As she began to understand and do better in her algebra class, she continued to feel she could still participate in all her activities.

After Thanksgiving the honor society tutor could no longer help Donna as she needed the time to fill out her own college applications. During the time between Thanksgiving break and Christmas break, Donna's grades in algebra dropped to failing. Donna began to realize even though she could do the math work, as evidenced by her ability to raise her grades when she had the tutor, she could not do it and still maintain her present lifestyle. She needed the discipline to sit down and concentrate. She appealed to the counselor for help in resolving this problem. The counselor began to see a break in Donna's attitude as Donna acknowledged that she needed to change her behavior patterns.

A plan was drawn up for Donna to make time for studying. She decided she would not try out for softball in the spring and would use that time to study and bring her overall grades up. Donna was concerned about telling her parents that she was not going to play softball. A meeting was arranged to present her decision to her parents. At the meeting Donna's parents were surprised and hurt that she had not confided in them. They felt she had been the one who chose to be constantly busy. They did not realize that she felt that her parents demanded the high activity level. The family redefined their goals.

The counselor continued to see Donna throughout the school year. Although Donna and her parents worked at improving her study habits and her priorities, on occasion she slipped, and periodically needed to recommit herself to her original plan. The counselor's support was crucial to Donna's eventual success.

COMPETENCY 11.0 Apply knowledge of group counseling principles and procedures

Skill 11.1 Merits and Limitations of Group Counseling

All major counseling theories can be applied to both individual and group counseling situations. During group counseling, the theories take on a more social nature. The theoretical method chosen depends upon the orientation of the counselor, the needs of the client(s), and the goals of the counseling process.

Merits of Group Counseling

In a group situation, members have the ability, in a safe and non-threatening atmosphere, to test their attitudes and beliefs against those of the other members of the group. They can receive feedback and discover how they are viewed by others. The group setting can also be a support system for its members, and may be particularly important when members have no other means of emotional support. In this way they can achieve and experiment with some of the goals of becoming emotionally involved without the threat of rejection.

A counseling group is made up of various members of society and thus can be a representation of the client's outer world – the world outside the counseling room. Members can experiment with their styles of interaction with other people in a contained, managed environment. They can then transfer these techniques and behaviors into real life situations. Members of the group can, as they process the observations of the group and their own reactions to others, get a better idea of who they want to become, as well as a better understanding of their own behavior.

For the counselor, the advantages of groups include the ability to reach more clients, to become familiar with differing populations of the school community, and to become more aware of current trends in youth culture.

Limitations of Group Counseling

There may be a tendency to view group counseling as a quick, easy solution when in fact the counselor may find that the work load preparation has increased in proportion to the number of members in the group. Often, individual members need different theoretical approaches as well as extended follow-up.
There is tremendous pressure to accept the group values and substitute them for the previous unworkable value system instead of forming new sets of approaches to the old problem.

Some people function poorly in the group situation. For one reason or another they cannot accept the group's perceptions and fall further into a psychological "funk". Some may find the group setting threatening in spite of the counselor's efforts to create a safe environment. Others have too many pressing issues to be able to focus in a group context. The personality or acute life circumstances of some individuals may prevent them from making changes in their lives. They may use the group to justify their present status and therefore do not gain from the group's insights.

An excellent resource on all aspects of group counseling is *The Theory and Practice of Group Psychotherapy* by Yalom and Leszcz (2005).

For more information about group counseling, see www.agpa.org/guidelines/factorsandmechanisms.html.

Skill 11.2 Group Dynamics

Understanding group dynamics is based on knowledge about the psychological and social forces inherent within groups. These forces operate in all human interactions. Over the last fifty years, the concept of group dynamics has become more developed and there exist a number of definitions of group dynamics.

One definition states that group dynamics is a political ideology that is built upon the concept of the organization and management of the group. It emphasizes democratic leadership, equality of membership in decision making and the benefits of group interaction to both society in general and the individual members specifically. Critics of this definition say the emphasis on the group is a method of operating rather than a way of understanding the goals and purpose of the group.

A second definition of group dynamics is derived from the techniques used in group process. Some of these techniques include role-playing, observation and feedback from group members, the decision making process and the concept of "buzz sessions". This type of group process was developed at the National Training Laboratory (www.ntl.org), among other places.

The third definition of group dynamics encompasses the entire field of research and application concerning the nature of groups, the history of their development and their interrelations with individuals, other groups and established institutions. This is the most accepted definition of group dynamics at this time, with a focus on human behavior and relationships.

School counselors have many opportunities to utilize knowledge of group dynamics. In the classroom setting, in group counseling, and in understanding the dynamics of peer groups, counselors can draw on understanding how groups affect individual students' behavior. Always being mindful of the power of groups to affect individuals can be an asset in many school counselor functions.

Some aspects of group dynamics especially relevant to group counseling settings include:

- Groups naturally progress through several stages of development. Different models describe different pathways, although they often show this pattern:
  - meeting and coming together
  - a struggle for power and acknowledgement of differences
  - overcoming the differences to allow intimacy and to work together
  - a process of individuals differentiating from the group
  - members moving on and ending or leaving the group

- All groups tend to develop patterns of communication and role distinction. These patterns tend to be emotionally charged with regard to conflict. These may or may be healthy, but awareness of these is commonly a part of the group process.

- Attending to the power dynamics operating within the group, including the overt or stated leader, as well as the informal or unstated leader, is important and informative. Different group members may exhibit power in different arenas at different points in time.

COMPETENCY 12.0 Apply knowledge of group guidance and principles

Skill 12.1 Developing Special Programs to Meet Identified Needs

Many group guidance activities emerge in response to particular needs. Although many of the school counselor's tasks are designated by the overall plan of the guidance program, there is occasionally the need to develop special programs to cope with an emerging problem or respond to a particular group of students. Such a need may be identified by a formal needs assessment or, more commonly, by a classroom management problem, teacher observations or direct knowledge of the counselor. A specific program to address the need can be a creative solution and serve to prevent an escalation of the problem.

Two examples of special programs are the Lunch Bunch and an anger management mini-group. The Lunch Bunch is an opportunity for new students to meet with other students new to the district and the counselor in a small group at lunch time. Meeting in a somewhat informal setting while eating lunch can be useful and non-threatening for new students. It addresses the discomfort some students feel at lunch time when long-time friends sit together. It helps build peer relationships as well as a connection with the school counselor. It can, after a few meetings, include "old" students to help the students build bridges into the larger school community. The Lunch Bunch should only meet short-term (4-6 times) once a week at the same time, in order to facilitate this process of integration.

A psycho-educational group focused on anger management can be an opportunity for violence and bullying prevention as well as an intervention strategy. In this setting (which is more formal than the Lunch Bunch, for example) the school counselor meets with a small group (6-8) of students who need help with anger management skills. They can be self-selected or identified by the counselor, teachers and other staff. In this group, skills are taught and information shared. Behavior modification approaches may also be employed. Further, students can discuss their concerns about and struggles with anger and other emotions.

Ideally, the school counselor has students complete evaluation forms following their involvement in such special programs, in order to assess their effectiveness. This information could be used in deciding to offer the program again, modifying the program or developing new programs. Other staff members and teachers who are involved in the program or are able to observe the effects of the program may also be solicited for their feedback.

Skill 12.2 Basic Prevention Concepts and Other Curricular Strategies

In addition to providing counseling after a problem has been identified, it is the task of the school counselor to contribute to the school's effort to prevent difficulties before they arise. Central to the notion of prevention is the importance of creating a positive school environment (see Skill 6.1). Further, as noted previously, attending to issues of bullying, prejudice, aggression and violence in the school setting are key to preventing problems. Teaching communication, self-awareness and conflict resolution skills to students are also effective prevention approaches.

Other key prevention concepts include the following ideas:

Maintain an open door policy. Students need to know that the school counselor is there to help. An attitude of openness and positive communication can encourage students to seek assistance when something concerns them before it escalates into a larger problem.

Create a student assistance team (SAP) By designating and training a group of teachers and staff (counselors, psychologist, nurse, social worker, etc.) as people students can go to when they are experiencing difficulties, the school offers students the opportunity to get the help they need to be successful in school. SAPs provide early intervention and referral, and have the advantage of being interdisciplinary and collaborative.

Implement programs that involve students in the school community in innovative ways. By engaging students in programs beyond the scope of the classroom and traditional guidance functions, they become invested in the larger school community. This enhances their self-esteem and helps forge new bonds among students. At times, peers are able to help students when adults are less able to do so. Attention needs to be given to recruitment of students for such programs, and adequate orientation, training and supervision must be provided.

Such programs might include the following:

1. **Cross-age teaching:** Have high school students help with programs for elementary and middle school students. These could involve tutoring, conflict resolution, peer mediation, or orientation for students moving from one school building to the next.

2. **New student welcoming committee:** Establish a group of students who are willing to mentor students new to the district. They can sit with their mentees at lunch and share information about the school. New friendships may develop, and both mentors and mentees have the chance to meet people who are perhaps different from them.

3. **Service clubs:** Sponsor or help start a service club oriented to helping students implement projects that improve the school and community environment. Some examples are a recycling project within the school, a holiday gift program for needy families, and a volunteer program to help the elderly in the community or to bring seasonal artwork to nursing home patients.

4. **Student involvement in the guidance program:** Inviting students to help out with guidance activities such as Career Day or Financial Aid Night or with office tasks can be worthwhile to students who are interested.

COMPETENCY 13.0 Understand referral procedures

Skill 13.1 Utilizing External Resources

One of the ongoing tasks of school counselors is to help students and families access and utilize resources outside the school setting. These connections may results from the counselor or other school personnel making the recommendation for referral, or it may occur when a student or parent/guardian asks for help or expressed a particular need.

Referrals to Outside Agencies and Practitioners

Appropriate referrals for students to professional individuals and agencies are procedural functions of both the school district and the specific school in which the counselor works. There is usually a set policy to which a referring school counselor must follow.

A form should be used to inform the person to whom the student is referred the nature of the problem, along with background information and standardized test scores, what has been tried already, with whom, and what the results are of different strategies employed. Follow-up and further meetings should be held to determine the outcome of the referral. The person to whom the student is referred should also issue a report on the results.

The first step in getting outside help for the student is to get the informed consent of the student and his/her parent/guardian to make the referral. In the case of abuse by a family or household member, the counselor is mandated to report the incident to the proper authorities as well. If a parent or guardian is the abuser it is not prudent to include that person in the referral process. The mandated state organization will approach the parent or guardian.

In the case of alcohol or other drug or emotional problems, the parent/guardian should be included from the start. The question of expense or insurance coverage is a significant factor to be considered. In any case of referral, written documentation should be kept. Personal contact with the agency receiving the referral should be made by the counselor. Regular contact with this individual and the parents should be made until the problem is resolved or the student is no longer enrolled in the school.

It is often helpful to have a form on which to track referrals to outside agencies and individuals. This creates a useful record for accountability purposes and makes follow-up easier.

Support and Resources for Families

The school counselor is often in the position of helping families access resources for purposes other than referrals for evaluative or mental health services. Sometimes the counselor will provide the student with information about resources; other times the counselor will offer referrals to the parents and guardians. Regardless, this requires knowledge of community and internet resources on many different topics including but not limited to financial aid, mental health and social service agencies, vocational training programs, food banks, prevention, support groups, colleges and universities, advocacy networks, government-sponsored aid programs, and enrichment activities.

Networking with community agencies, private practitioners, other school districts, professional associations and local and state education agencies can be useful in gathering resource information. The counselor should maintain a database as well as a file of brochures, business cards and information packets to draw on as needed. It is also helpful to keep a list of contact people at various agencies and programs in order to facilitate referrals and expedite access for families.

TEACHER CERTIFICATION STUDY GUIDE

COMPETENCY 14.0 Understand intervention procedures

Skill 14.1 Core Crisis Intervention Concepts and Approaches

Crisis and emergency situations are events beyond the realm of every day life. They always involve some degree of surprise, shock, loss and emotion. Crises include death, natural disasters such as earthquakes and hurricanes, vehicular and other accidents, school shootings, and other forms of extreme violence. The unpredictability of crises, the experience of loss that invariably accompanies such situations and the strong feelings that are evoked all make crisis and emergency events particularly potent and challenging for everyone involved.

The value of being prepared

Pre-planning and training in basic crisis management skills can be extremely helpful in responding effectively. Although the events themselves may be unpredictable, there is a body of information about how people react to crisis and what responders can do to ameliorate and manage the aftermath of crisis. This is important in school settings, where there are a large number of people congregated in one place and contagion is a concern. Anxiety and misinformation can spread like wildfire, exacerbating the short and long term effects of traumatic events.

Designating and training a crisis response team can be quite beneficial. Comprehensive crisis management training as well as ongoing refresher courses are necessary for a team to function well. In most cases, the school counselor is integrally involved in the work of crisis team. He or she may be a leader or not, depending on the structure of the team, the preferences of the administration, and the background of the counselor.

In addition to a crisis team, school districts need to have clearly defined crisis response plans. They should include as much detail as possible, with specific recommendations for different situations as needed, although a general plan is applicable in many circumstances. The plan should incorporate the following:

- delineate the school's goals in crisis situations (such as maintaining as normal a school day as possible, or providing timely information),
- identify key players on the crisis response team,
- specify how communication will be handled,
- describe what interventions will be used with students,
- note how interactions and referrals to outside agencies will be managed,
- detail what follow-up is needed.

Further, it helps to have handouts about traumatic stress reactions, sample letters to parents and guardians, press releases (when necessary) and other useful documents ready prior to any event.

The need for information

Everyone who experiences a traumatic event needs to be aware of the normal reactions and common feelings of survivors, as well as receive accurate information about the event itself (when this is not known) and what the school is doing in response. This means that the district needs to make clear decisions about the actions the school is taking, including what parents and guardians need to know and do, and communicate these plans succinctly and in a timely manner to all in the school community. Information also needs to flow to the larger community. Specific, to-the-point information is valuable; avoid all rumors.

Intervention for students

Most commonly, school counselors and other school personnel will be available for crisis counseling and support in a designated room for a day or two after a traumatic event. Some districts will invite local experts in traumatic stress response or grief counseling to come to the school to aid school personnel. Interventions include listening, normalizing the reactions of students, offering to call parents and guardians, and making arrangements for the student to go home early when needed. Referrals to outside professionals may also be made.

Self-care during and after the event

Part of a school crisis plan should spell out how responders and other school personnel will receive and give support during the implementation of the crisis management plan. Further, school counselors and other personnel need to get rest and support after doing crisis response work. This work is very demanding and the effects on responders may not be immediately apparent. Secondary post-traumatic stress is a concern, particularly when the crisis response team has multiple or ongoing situations to manage. Adequate administrative and personal support, time off, and sufficient training and de-briefing are essential.

The following websites have information about school crisis management, traumatic stress reactions, and related topics:

www.nctsnet.org/nccts/nav.do?pid=ctr_aud_schlmeans that part of the crisis response
 www.cdc.gov/niosh/unp-trinstrs.html
 www.aaets.org/trresp.htm
www.apa.org/practice/traumaticstress.html
www.ed.gov/admins/lead/safety/training/responding/crisis_pg11.html?exp=2.

Skill 14.2 The School Counselor as Advocate

An advocate is someone who speaks up for another (usually someone lacking power in a situation) with the goal of making sure that person is heard. Schools are complex systems comprised of many individuals and groups competing for resources and attention. At times, students and/or parents and guardians may not feel their concerns are being acknowledged or addressed. Counselors may also observe ongoing issues with groups of students, or recognize segments of the student body who are not receiving adequate support or services. In these circumstances, there may be a need for someone to advocate for these individuals or groups.

School counselors are in a unique position to serve as an advocate for students. They do not grade or evaluate students' academic performance, and they do not function as disciplinarian for the school. Nor are they in the position of decision-maker regarding school policies that might affect individual students and families.

Further, they may be privy to students' personal concerns, and have the training and background to understand some of the underlying issues and needs of diverse students. Parents and guardians may also feel that the school counselor is more open to discussing their concerns than other school personnel may be.

Being an advocate requires listening carefully. After hearing someone's concerns or identifying an issue, advocacy requires a frank discussion about what kind of help the student or parent/guardian wants. The school counselor needs to assess the appropriateness of the request for this kind of help and determine a good action plan. (See Competencies 25 and 26 for more information.)

In setting goals to advocate for an individual or a group, the advocate needs to ensure that his or her own personal agenda is not driving the need to speak up. Passion about an issue can be valuable, even necessary at times, to effecting change, but taking action on someone's behalf needs to be grounded in accurately assessing the issues at hand and advocating in a professional manner. A good advocate not only speaks with a strong, compassionate voice but is also able to bring clear thinking, a collaborative attitude, and respectful communication to the table.

COMPETENCY 15.0 Understand the needs of students with special concerns (e.g., at-risk students, students with personal or family problems)

Skill 15.1 Child Abuse and Neglect

Governmental and nongovernmental sources report that between 12 and 15 children out of every thousand children are abused each year by immediate family members or people living in the home. This does not include abuse and violence perpetrated by others outside the home. Also, these numbers reflect only reported cases of abuse. Abuse or neglect may occur for years before it is investigated; in other cases, abuse continues unchecked. Many children are fearful about reporting abuse for a range of reasons, including the desire to protect one's caregivers and worry about the consequences of reporting.

Given the prevalence of abuse and neglect, it is important the counselor recognizes potential signs of child abuse and neglect. When behavioral indicators are present, counselors should meet with students individually to gather more information about suspected abuse, and to determine who in the child's family or network can be an ally. (See Skill 21.3 for information on reporting child abuse and neglect.)

The easiest type of abuse to detect is *physical abuse.* Unexplained bruises, bite marks, burns, fractures and other physical indicators suggest that a child has been physically abused. In addition the child can exhibit withdrawal and aggressive behavior, self-destructive behavior, self-injury (such as sticking a pencil into parts of the body or pinching oneself), and avoidance of physical contact with others.

Child neglect is indicated by an unattended need for medical care, reported lack of supervision, dirty unkempt and generally poor hygiene, as well as always being hungry. Common behavioral manifestations are falling asleep inappropriately, stealing food, frequent absences, expressions of hunger and self-destructive behaviors.

For the child who has been *sexually abused* there may be some difficulty in sitting or walking, stained clothing, venereal disease and pain or itching in the genital area. The behavioral manifestations can be quite varied. Overtly sexualized behavior in children under the age of 12 may be an indicator, as can attention problems in school work, self-injury, depression, extremely volatile emotions, suicidal thoughts or gestures, and an inability to control one's behavior in children of all ages.

For the *emotionally abused* child the indicators are eating disorders, sleeping problems, loss of energy and chronic complaints. The behavior manifestations include depression, low self-esteem, lack of self confidence, poor peer relations, and suicidal thoughts or gestures.

The Center for Disease Control has information about child abuse and neglect at www.cdc.gov/ncipc/dvp/CMP/default.htm. Information about child sexual abuse is also available at www.nlm.nih.gov/medlineplus/childsexualabuse.html.

Skill 15.2 Substance Abuse and Addiction

Many students and families are impacted by chemical addiction. School counselors need to have some basic information about drug and alcohol use and abuse. Many resources are available in the form of books and pamphlets as well as on the internet regarding addiction; local treatment programs and rehabilitation centers are often willing to provide in-service training programs for guidance staff and can also provide free literature.

The job of the school counselor is to recognize the signs of addiction and substance abuse in students and, with the cooperation of the student's parent/guardians, make referrals to the proper agency for treatment. Students may need residential care; other times an outpatient or partial hospital program is adequate. It is the counselor's job to follow-up with the treatment provider, and facilitate the transition of the student back into the school setting as needed. Some of the indicators of substance abuse in students are:

- An inability to perform at school and home in spite of apparent cognitive capacity and the lack of other interfering factors.
- Excessive sleepiness or irritability.
- Mood swings or seeming personality changes.
- Secretive behavior.
- Sudden change in friends.
- Use of substances in dangerous situations despite the possibility of physical harm, such as driving a motor vehicle or swimming.
- Continued use that results in legal problems such as prosecution for drunken driving, arrests for disturbing the peace and possession of a controlled substance.
- Inability to stop using the controlled substance in spite of social problems such as fights, conflict with family and peers, and poor school performance.

Denial is not uncommon when confronting a student with a substance abuse problem. It may be effective for the school to require the student to attend alcohol and/or drug counseling before returning to school if there has been a breach of school rules and policies by the student. A referral to a professional in the drug abuse field for an evaluation is always an appropriate action when counselors are concerned about the possibility of abuse or addiction.

Parental Substance Abuse

Some students are affected by their parent or guardian's use or abuse of drugs and alcohol; they may or may not be users themselves. Many of the indicators of addiction in the home are similar to other stress indicators, such as poor school performance, anxiety, avoidance of intimacy, depression, guilt and over-responsibility. For more information about students with substance-abusing parents see www.puberty101.com/aacap_alcoholc.shtml and kidshealth.org/teen/your_mind/families/coping_alcoholic.html.

General online resources about substance abuse and addiction include www.drugabuse.gov/parent-teacher.html, www.niaaa.nih.gov/FAQs/General-English/default.htm, and www.adolescent-substance-abuse.com/signs-drug-use.html.

Skill 15.3 Suicide, Self-Injury, Eating Disorders and Interpersonal Violence

The problems of suicide, anorexia, bulimia, sexual assault, dating violence and self-injury are serious, often long term counseling problems beyond the scope of a school counselor's duties. They may require that the counselor communicate with a range of community agencies and personnel. The school counselor's primary tasks are identification, crisis counseling, parental notification, referral, support, and follow up. It is essential that the counselor utilize the school's protocol in these instances, and report the information to school administration. It may also be appropriate for the school counselor to involve the student assistance team within the school setting.

The American Psychiatric Association notes on their webpage for **teen suicide** that although "...the teen suicide rate has declined by over 25 percent since the early 1990s, suicide is the third leading cause of death among young people ages 15 to 24." (See www.healthyminds.org/multimedia/teensuicide.pdf.)

They go on to detail the following statistics about teen suicide:

> • It is estimated that depression increases the risk of a first suicide attempt by at least 14-fold.
> • Over half of all kids who suffer from depression will eventually attempt suicide at least once, and more than seven percent will die as a result.
> • Four times as many men commit suicide than women, but young women attempt suicide three times more frequently than young men.
> • Fifty-three percent of young people who commit suicide abuse substances.
> • Firearms are used in a little more than half of all youth suicides."

One of the most common and effective methods school personnel have to recognize the suicidal student is in the writings of that student. Often, an English teacher will come to the counselor with a sample of a student's writing that suggests thoughts and/or plans of suicide. Other times, the counselor may learn that the student is thinking about suicide by comments made directly by the student, or from friends of the student who are concerned.

When such information comes to the attention of the counselor, the counselor should meet as soon as possible with the student. If the student is known to the counselor and a rapport has been built, it is appropriate to speak directly with the student, with the teacher's permission, about the material of concern. Even if the counselor does not already have a relationship with the student, sometimes the counselor must proceed without a prior connection and work at building rapport in the moment.

If confirmation of the suicidal intent is received from the student (and in many cases, even if the student does not confirm suicidal intent), the counselor has a duty to inform the parent/guardian(s), the school administration and the school nurse, that the student is currently at risk. Plans for intervention should be made at the time of this discovery. Do not delay until the next day, or until after a weekend. Once the parent/guardian(s) and/or appropriate professionals are notified, the treatment is in the hands of those who have the skills and authority to deal with the problem.

Self-injury is not uncommon in adolescents and sometimes occurs in middle school students as well. Self-injury is direct harm to the body, such as cutting or burning; it is distinguished from a suicide attempt in that the intent behind the self-injury is *not* connected to a wish to die. Self-injury serves to release tension and help the student manage emotional pain and distress. The counselor may learn about such behavior by direct observation (scars, wounds, bandages) or from the student engaging in self-injury or their friends. Like eating disorders, addressing this issue is a long term problem and requires referral to appropriate mental health professionals. However, school counselors may be in the position of providing support to teen who self-injure as well as offering information and referral.

For more information about self-injury, go to www.healingselfinjury.org/.

Anorexia nervosa, where someone starves him / herself, or its variant, **bulimia**, where the person alternately binges on food and then purges by vomiting or using laxatives, are eating disorders that also arise particularly in adolescence. Again, the counselor may recognize the problem by direct observation and/or reports from the student's friends and peers. Addressing these problems with students can be difficult because the student often truly believes he/she is overweight, or has normal eating patterns.

Eating disorders are often associated with depression and low self-esteem, and, unchecked, can lead to malnutrition, body chemistry imbalance, cessation of the menstrual cycle and other endocrine dysfunctions.

See kidshealth.org/parent/nutrition_fit/nutrition/eating_disorders.html for more information, warning signs, and resources for coping with eating disorders in teens.

Intervening with Students about Self-Injury, Suicide and Eating Disorders

When a counselor learns that a student may have an eating disorder, is self-injuring, or is thought to be at risk for suicide, s/he needs to meet with the student to explore the student's perceptions and concerns. It is also the professional responsibility of the counselor along with the school nurse and other medical school personnel to inform the parent/guardian(s). The parent/guardian needs to be aware of the problem and may also need information, support and encouragement in seeking help for their child from the appropriate medical or mental health professional. The school's student assistance team might also be useful in aiding with referral, support, and follow up.

Interpersonal violence is another common problem among teens. One in three teenagers experiences dating violence (www.acadv.org/dating.html) and a number of teens are also raped or sexually assaulted by either an acquaintance or stranger. The issue of interpersonal physical or sexual violence is likely to be brought to school counselors along with the psychological issues noted above. It is not unusual for the friends of students who are being abused to come to the counselors or teachers. Reports of such situations require the same sensitivity and attention that other serious issues demand, including contact with parent/guardian(s) and appropriate referrals. These cases may also require the involvement of law enforcement personnel.

COMPETENCY 16.0 Understand issues related to the needs of students from all cultural backgrounds

Skill 16.1 Cultural Competence

School counselors have a duty and responsibility to become attuned to the specific needs and issues relevant to all socio-cultural groups represented in their school district and community. Without such attunement, counselors are not able to adequately provide school guidance services to some students and families. In order to be effective across many cultural groups, school counselors must develop cultural competence and cross-cultural communication skills.

Developing cultural competence does not happen overnight or simply by attending a training workshop on the topic. It is an ongoing process of self-reflection, learning and skill development. Developing an understanding of one's own values, attitudes and awareness of diversity is a first step. Moving beyond cultural sensitivity to cultural competence in a school setting involves learning about other cultural beliefs and attitudes, particularly in relation to schools and institutions, and then developing skills that enable the counselor to relate and communicate well with people of differing socio-cultural backgrounds.

One area that is important to understand is the significance of cross-cultural interactions: how different groups have historically interacted with each other, especially within the context of institutions such as schools and health care systems. Many minority groups, especially people of color, have been mistreated by and underrepresented in many societal institutions. These negative experiences and the resulting distrust can make cross-cultural communication challenging for school counselors at times.

Acquiring cross-cultural skills aimed at respect, trust-building, and effective communication is essential in achieving cultural competence. Further, institutional policies and practices need to be changed as well. Minority groups need to be represented at all levels of the school administration and staff to reach cultural competence. Although this level of change is beyond the scope of the school counselor's role, counselors may be in a position to advocate for policy and practice change. An example of this is adapting practices to better accommodate and respond to the cultural needs of students and families. By doing this on a case-by-case basis and then presenting this information to administrators may allow for change to occur at the institutional level.

Two websites that offer more detailed information about cultural competence are cecp.air.org/cultural/default.htm and www11.georgetown.edu/research/gucchd/nccc/foundations/frameworks.html.

Skill 16.2 Bullying, Stereotyping and Prejudice

A lack of respect for diversity is often evidenced by bullying behavior. Increasing, schools are finding they need to take action to address stereotyping, prejudice and bullying among students. A number of factors lead to bullying behavior. Stereotypes and prejudice are major contributors, along with personal characteristics and life experiences of the bullying student. These may include poor social skills, distorted self-perceptions, problems with aggression and impulse control, and previous victimization experiences.

Certain characteristics and personality traits of other individuals may serve as magnets for prejudice and stereotyping. Some of these targets are based on membership in a specific group such as gender, race, ethnicity, religion, physical ability, sexual orientation, and age. Stereotypes abound in our culture regarding these characteristics, and these stereotypes are frequently brought into the school setting and used as the basis for teasing and bullying.

However, such stereotypes are not the only source of bias. Anything that makes a person different in the eyes of the perceiver – anything out of the "norm" – can trigger ridicule, ostracism, hate and violence. Some of these perceptual biases are:

- attractiveness vs. unattractiveness
- thin vs. obese individuals
- effeminate males vs. virile males
- masculine females vs. feminine females
- "in" group vs. "out" group (i.e., cool vs. not-cool)

The presence of difference, in and of itself, is not a problem in the larger world or the school setting. In fact, in a positive school environment, such differences are acknowledged and appreciated. The important issue, however, is the way individuals who are perceived as different are treated, and how that treatment affects the social and emotional well-being of the targeted individuals.

There is evidence to suggest that the self-esteem of a student is directly affected by this type of stereotyping. The stereotyping and its effects can begin as early as the first time a child enters school and may continue throughout the life span.

As a result of excessive teasing or bullying, the targeted individual may:

1. Believes there is something wrong with them and considers him/herself a "loser."
2. Develops emotional problems connected with the perceived inferiority.
3. Manifests a lack of motivation and desire to excel as "It doesn't matter what I do as I never do anything right."
4. Displays personality problems.

5. Begins to feel life isn't worth living and contemplates suicide.
6. Begins to harbor thoughts of violence against the perpetrators of the perceived insult.
7. In extreme cases, carries out an act of self-violence or violence against others.

If not educated to accept differences among people, the perpetrator of the stereotyping, prejudice or other bullying type activities is likely to:

1. Escalate the activity.
2. Enlist others to engage in the activity.
3. Become firm in their beliefs that the targeted individual is undesirable.
4. Feel superior to the targeted individual or groups and justify his/her actions.
5. Become resistant to changing attitudes and incorporate them into a way of life.
6. Resort to violence after justifying the violence in his/her mind.

Programs to combat stereotyping, prejudice and biases should be part of the school curriculum. Although the labeling of entire groups of people is irrational, the school must respond rationally and create programs to address with these issues. Students can be taught to respect the rights of others by programs of cooperation and conflict resolution.

A good website for students as well as teachers and counselors on bullying prevention can be found at **stopbullyingnow.hrsa.gov/index.asp**.

Skill 16.3 Aggression, Violence, and Conflict Resolution

In 2005, the federal Centers for Disease Control and Prevention did a national survey of high school students' risk behaviors and reported this information in relation to school violence:

• 13.6% reported being in a physical fight on school property in the 12 months preceding the survey.

• 18.2% of male students and 8.8% of female students reported being in a physical fight on school property in the 12 months preceding the survey.

• 29.8% of students reported having property stolen or deliberately damaged on school property.

• 6.0% did not go to school on one or more days in the 30 days preceding the survey because they felt unsafe at school or on their way to or from school.

• 6.5% reported carrying a weapon (gun, knife or club) on school property on one or more days in the 30 days preceding the survey.

• 7.9% reported being threatened or injured with a weapon on school property one or more times in the 12 months preceding the survey."

(Source: www.cdc.gov/ncipc/dvp/YV_DataSheet.pdf)

We are all familiar with the school shootings that occur once in a while. However, the above data reflect the equally troubling and perhaps more relevant facts regarding everyday violence in schools. A major factor contributing to violence in schools is the acceptance of violence as a "normal" reaction to perceived injustices. Media depictions of violence may convey a perception that violent retaliation is "normal" and common. Easy access to guns and other weapons, and the effect of both drug abuse and the way the drug culture permeates the larger culture also may contribute to school violence.

In the school setting, administrators, teachers, counselors and support staff have the responsibility to make the school a safe place for all students. Clear policies that delineate safety and guide behavior are useful in working toward this goal. Policies should articulate appropriate behavior on school property and at school events with regard to the following topics, as well as others:

1. Weapons
2. Homicidal and/or suicidal intent
3. Use of drugs and alcohol
4. Self-harm
5. Sexual harassment
6. Bullying
7. Violent threats

However, policies are not enough. Preventing violence and resolving conflicts in interpersonal relations are fundamentally related. Programs of violence prevention must be accompanied by programs of constructive conflict resolution so student can learn methods of positive interactions with others, including those who are different. Not only do these programs help create a safe environment in the schools, but they also teach students the skills to resolve future conflicts in their careers, family, and community as adults. A program of violence prevention and conflict resolution acknowledges that while destructive and violent conflicts may be out of control in our society we can strive to minimize them in any particular school, home or other setting.

The conflict resolution program should:

1. Create an atmosphere of cooperation.
2. Have a component of peer meditation training that teaches negotiation, mediation and arbitration skills to students and teachers.
3. Include units in academic classes on methods of negotiation, mediation and arbitration.

Active violence prevention programs include:

1. The elimination of weapons in school by metal detectors, random locker searches and appropriate personnel to monitor the open school areas.
2. A law enforcement presence on the surrounding property of the school for monitoring and enforcement purposes.
3. Training programs for faculty and staff so they are better able to recognize and intervene before and during violent confrontations.
4. A system for identifying students who are or are at risking of becoming perpetrators of violence and refer them to behavior modification, anger management or other appropriate programs.
5. The creation of a district task force to identify and address the causes of violence in the school district.
6. Effective policies addressing violent behavior and a program that assures student protection if they feel they are in danger.
7. Counseling and/or referral for students traumatized by violence.

Bullying and violence prevention resources are available at **www.cdc.gov/ncipc/dvp/YVP/YVP-data.htm** and **mentalhealth.samhsa.gov/15plus/aboutbullying.asp**.

The National Youth Violence Prevention Resource Center offers resources not only on bullying and violence prevention but also addresses substance abuse and other safety issues for teens at www.safeyouth.org/scripts/topics/school.asp.

Subarea: **EDUCATIONAL AND CAREER PLANNING**

COMPETENCY 17.0 Apply procedures for determining educational placement in relation to career goals

Skill 17.1 Educational Placement and Career Goals

Course Options and Scheduling

School counselors are intimately involved in helping students schedule their coursework at middle and high school level. Even elementary school counselors may be in a position to help students and parent/guardian(s) make choices about academic pathways and elective courses. The process of course selection is an ongoing process throughout the student's years at school.

It is essential that counselors are familiar with their school's curriculum and have a good grasp of the basic schedule, as well as prerequisites and other special requirements for certain courses. They must understand the links between various academic tracks and courses as they relate to different career and postsecondary education options. Equally crucial is an awareness of each student's interests, abilities, and prior coursework along with any relevant assessment data.

Each district has procedures that outline how students may sign up for courses, including parental approval. Some districts have strict policies about admission into certain classes, such as advanced placement or higher level courses. Some schools also offer cross-education with local colleges and universities, as well as with vocational and technical schools. Counselors need to be familiar with all the options available to students interested in a range of careers and educational pathways.

Individualized Education Plans (IEP)

A number of students will also have individualized education plans. These may be students with cognitive impairment, learning problems, physical disabilities, social or emotional issues, or some other exceptionality. School counselors are not solely responsible for developing these plans but are part of a team that may involve the school psychologist, the school nurse, special education teachers and administrators, the school social worker, the parent/guardian(s), and/or outside service providers. School counselors need to be familiar with each student's IEP and adhere to the school district's procedures regarding their role in the implementation of the IEP.

COMPETENCY 18.0 Apply knowledge of approaches for and theories of career development and occupational choice

Skill 18.1 Similarities and Differences of Career Development Theories

There are five different classifications or methods of approach into which most major career counseling theories fall:

1) trait-factor theories
2) societal circumstances of career choice theory
3) developmental theories
4) personality and vocational choice theories and
5) environmental behavioral influences on career choice theories

The **trait-factor theories** assume there is a direct relationship between an individual's interests and abilities and vocational choices. When these are matched, the individual has found their future vocation. Interest inventories, aptitude tests and the general field of vocational testing have been generated from this theory.

The **societal circumstances of career choice theory** contend that circumstances of society, beyond the control of the individual, are the contributing factor in career choice. In this theory, the only control the individual has is in learning to cope with the environment.

The **developmental or self-concept theory** holds that as an individual grows older self-concept changes along with the view of the reality of his/her vocational choice. The satisfaction derived from the chosen career is based upon the individual's self-concept and the relation of self-concept to the vocational choice.

The **personality and vocational choice theories** are based upon the concept that people of like personalities choose the same types of vocations. The needs of like personalities are the same and therefore they select the same vocations to satisfy those needs. The research done in this area has studied individuals who are already in a specific field as the norm group; their personalities are compared to those wishing to enter the field.

The **environmental behavior theory** incorporates elements of the societal circumstance and personality theories into a classification system that observes the relationship between the interaction of individuals in the environment and their behavior.

Most theorists in career development borrow from each other in formulating their theories. Some of key concepts of the most enduring theories follow:

1. **Bordin**, **Nachmann**, and **Segal** developed a framework for vocational development using a psychoanalytic theory base. By using the occupations of accounting, social work, and plumbing they attempted to generalize a system that might be used to classify occupations into areas of psychoanalytic dimensions.

2, **Ginzberg**, **Ginzberg**, **Axelrad** and **Herma** developed a theory that vocational choice is divided into three stages. The **fantasy period** is characterized by the lack of reality of the child in vocational choice. It is based on the child's imaginings and interests. The **tentative period** is characterized by a shift from the child's *interests* as they become aware that they have more *capacities* in one area than another. They then begin to consider these abilities in vocational choice. As they become older they begin to consider the *value* or satisfaction they get from some activities over others, and in the final stage they begin to incorporate all these subdivisions into the *transition period and* move into the **realistic period.** This period is divided into the *exploration stage* when all the elements of the tentative period are incorporated, with the added insight of what is feasible for the individual. These results come together in the *crystallization stage* that finally leads to the *stage of specification* where the individual finally makes a choice of a specific occupation. The theory is based on the general concepts of developmental psychology.

3. **Holland**'s theory of vocational personalities and work environments is based upon the individual's adjustment to six occupational environments and the interaction of those environments to the personalities of individuals.

The first of these six **occupational environments/personality types** is described as (1) *realistic*, portrayed by individuals who deal better with things than ideas or people, are oriented towards the present, and value tangible things such as money, power, and status. They avoid dealing with subjectivity and intellectualism, and lack social skills. They are persistent, mature and simple. These people are in the occupations of engineering, technical fields, skilled trades and agriculture.

The (2) *investigative* person thinks, organizes, understands, and copes with problems intellectually. They think themselves as intellectuals and scholars and tend to avoid interpersonal relationships. Their achievement is in academic and scientific areas. They hold less conventional attitudes and are found in occupations related to math and science.

The (3) *social* personality seeks satisfaction in therapeutic situations and is skilled in close interpersonal relations. They are sensitive to the needs of others. They are involved in teaching, understanding others, helping others by using their verbal and social skills for behavior changes, and are optimistic, scholarly and verbally oriented. They are found in the helping occupations.

The (4) *conventional* personality values rules and regulations, has a great deal of self-control, is neat and organized, and needs structure and order. They think of themselves as conforming and orderly. They identify with power and status but do not necessarily aspire to obtain those for themselves. They follow orders well. They are found in accounting, business and clerical vocations.

(5) Enterprising individuals are skilled verbally but use these skills for manipulation and domination and aspire to obtain power and status. They are aggressive, self-confident, verbal and social. Political, leadership and power roles are important to them and they aspire to obtain these roles. They are found in occupations of sales, supervision and leadership.

Finally the (6) *artistic* personality relates with others through artistic expression, dislikes structure, and relies on feelings and imagination. They think of themselves as intuitive, introspective, nonconforming, and independent. They value artistic qualities and are not interested in politics. They relate by the use of their artistic abilities. They are found in the arts, music, literature and creative areas.

The characteristics of the environments the above personalities seek closely resemble their traits and therefore dominate the work environment. It follows then that people seek out the work environments that suit their personalities.

4. **Roe** developed the concept that every individual inherits certain ways of expending their energies. This, combined with childhood experiences, results in a style that manifests itself in vocational choices. She draws on the needs theory of Maslow (webspace.ship.edu/cgboer/maslow.html) as well. The concept of genetic disposition together with needs theory and the influence of childhood experiences and innate style come together to form the basis of vocational choice.

5. **Super**'s theory of vocational behavior is based on the development of a vocational self-concept. This theory emerges from developmental psychology and behavior theory in relation to self-concept. He proposes that people express their self-concepts by entering occupations they perceive to allow self-expression. Individuals behavior in order to enhance their self-concept; different behaviors occur as a result of their present stage of life development. As the individual matures the self-concept becomes stable, but external conditions contribute to how that self-concept is expressed vocationally.

Super explored the developmental life stages of the individual in reference to vocational behavior. These stages are similar to Ginzberg's classifications. They include *crystallization, specification, implementation, stabilization*, and, finally, *consolidation.* The adolescent is in the explorer stage in search of a career direction, the young adult seeks job training and job seeking, and the mature adult finds a vocation and secures a position.

6. **Tiedman** and his colleagues saw career development as a result of the developing self. The components include situational, societal and biological factors. The decision making process involves anticipation, implementation and adjustment. The sequence is characterized by an initial level of disorganized thinking about vocations, followed by clearer thinking and then evaluation of the advantages, disadvantages and values of each vocation. Teidman believes career decisions evolve from the links between work and non-work activities.

There are many similarities in the theories of vocational choice:

1. Most of the theories are constructive; they use two sets of observations to describe the relationship between the person and vocational choice.

2. The theories are generally descriptive rather than explanatory.

3. There is a great similarity in their explanations.

4. The research has not been experimental. Rather, these theories sort by groups and predict vocational choice based on characteristics of that group.

5. Most of the theories have roots in personality theory.

6. The theories are generally simple and uncomplicated.

There are also some differences:

1. Each of the theories states a particular set of objectives the individual is trying to accomplish through vocational choice.

2. Some theories have sufficient empirical data to support them and others have little empirical support.

3. There is a difference in when the most significant experiences for career development occur and what the critical sources of influence are.

4. The role of aptitudes is given various degrees of influence on career choice by the different theorists.

5. The role of family influence on career choice is treated with varying degrees of importance.

Generally the similarities among the theories are greater than the differences. They emphasize the same types of critical periods in career development and have their roots in personality theory. The differences lie in the choice of emphasis, the research methods appropriate for use in each theory, and the degree to which the relationship between various events occur.

COMPETENCY 19.0 Understand career development and information programs

Skill 19.1 Strategies for Developing Employability Skills

Attitude and Motivation

When students succeed in their studies they are eager to continue their education. They are more likely, too, to understand the relationship between the acquisition of education and their future lifestyles. When students do not succeed it is very difficult for them to see the value of education and how it relates to their future. When basic survival is demanding the student's attention, and the student does poorly in school, and the tendency to drop out of school or to engage in illicit profitable activities, such as crime and drug dealing, has a fatal attraction.

Counselors can help students facing these challenges to marshal resources to cope with life, as well as help them learn to defer present wants and needs (and peer pressure) in order to receive enhanced rewards at a later date. Further, these students may need specific support regarding academic achievement such as tutoring or special classes.

Exposure to role models who have escaped from poverty and/or crime is important for some students. Persuading such role models to mentor unmotivated students, and providing satisfying educational opportunities in the school may help students explore their potential more fully. Innovative programs can be found by using the resources of the community, the cooperation of parents and the resources of the school. There is also the availability of grant monies to implement programs for unmotivated students in some settings.

Throughout a student's high school career the opportunity to relate subject matter to career and job opportunities should be included in the curriculum of each subject. Job fairs and other types of exposure to job requirements should be presented to students at every opportunity.

An additional method of motivating students to acquire employable skills is to engage community businesses in making a commitment to employ students who adequately prepare themselves for entrance into the job market of the sponsoring business or industry. Apprenticeships, internships and supervised employment while still in school, as a requirement for graduation in a particular area, will encourage students to acquire the skills needed to go from high school graduation to a job that is waiting for them.

When students have incentives they are more likely to work at acquiring the math, English, science and technical skills required by the employer. They will also work at studying other subject areas in which they are not as interested in order to obtain the requirements needed for graduation. When they are working in satisfying positions, they can then have a concrete opportunity to see the need for future education; they may also be able to get their tuition paid for by their employer.

Developing Job-Seeking Skills

Helping students develop the skills they need to seek and secure a job is critical, particularly at the high school level. While some of these skills may be taught directly by the school counselor, collaborative efforts with teachers in English, social sciences and other disciplines may be most productive. These teachers can incorporate skill development opportunities into the curriculum, with input from the guidance department.

Some of the areas that may be included are:

- Resume writing

- Filling out job applications

- How to read the want ads

- How to search online for jobs

- Interviewing skills, including how to dress, how to prepare, and appropriate follow-up after the interview

Skill 19.2 Exploring Education and Career Options

There are many methods of exploring careers and the educational options open to students. They include computer-generated career inventories, career and educational search materials, and detailed information about specific careers and training requirements. The role of the counselor is to help students gather data so they make intelligent, informed and realistic choices. This entails providing information in a timely fashion at the appropriate developmental stage, and following through with support to explore possibilities.

Computer Generated Career Inventories and Search Procedures

Computer assisted advising can very useful to students, counselors and others involved in helping students with educational and career decision. **CHOICES** is one commercial system that is available to help students explore and research different vocational and career choices. Other career exploration programs include **Discover, Career Information Systems (CIS), Coordinate Occupational Information Network (COIN), Guidance Information System (GIS),** and **Systems of Interactive Guidance and Information (SIGI)**.

These programs can give students the ability to hone in on the occupations suited to their personality and fitting with their academic achievement and interests. It is the responsibility of the counselor to become familiar with any network or program, and to teach the student how to access the material. It is also the counselor's responsibility to help the student sift through the data and further explore selected occupations through other means.

Career Day

Community resources are always available to aid the counselor in presenting real life career situations. The organization of the career day program is a time-consuming activity but it offers many opportunities for both the student and the counselor. The counselor makes valuable contacts in the community for future jobs for the students, for creating business relationships to help students and for enhancing the image of the school. Community business institutions are eager to influence young people to enter their professions in order to create a pool of future applicants. The student gathers a wealth of occupational information and can hone in on the areas of most interest. The students can also make their own contacts and make arrangements with businesspeople for further contacts. The counselor should take care to have a representative from each career cluster in order to draw students of varying abilities and interests.

Job Shadowing

Shadowing is the process of spending an extended period of time with a particular person in a field that interests the student as a possible future career. The student does not have to be fully committed to pursuing this career, but should have narrowed down the choices to a few specific careers so to make the best use of everyone's time. The student should be given a set of rules to follow when choosing to participate and a form to fill out for an evaluation of the experience.

The community businessperson should also fill out a form prior to students engaging in job shadowing. Questions such as what the business expects to get from the experience, how much time they are willing to spend with the student and their general practices should be included in the questionnaire. The business should also fill out an evaluation after the student has completed the shadowing experience. A bad experience on the part of the community volunteer might lead that person to not participate in the program the following year, and the counselor needs to know how the process went from the volunteer's perspective.

School-to-Work Programs

One of the best ways to teach students to develop employability skills is to have the student participate in a supervised job experience. Motivation for the student to participate in this type of activity would be to incorporate it into the vocational curriculum and award high school credit to the student for successful completion of this component. Such school-to-work programs can be very useful.

Basic information about effective functioning in the world of work should be conveyed to the student. These include getting to the job on time, avoiding absences for all reasons other than illness, and calling the employer if one is ill and cannot report to work. Many students do not understand the importance of appearance and personal hygiene in obtaining and maintaining a job. These are basics that often have to be taught. In addition, many students have an attitude problem that has been carried over from school. Students need to understand that such attitudes are not tolerated in employment situations.

The instructional component of the school-to-work program should contain extensive material for the evaluation of the student by the employer as to attitude, work habits, personal hygiene, and attendance, as well as knowledge of the job and the ability and willingness to learn and be taught. Weekly work evaluation sheets completed by the employee and the employer show what the student has learned and done well, as well as areas that need improvement. Many school-to-work programs provide these evaluation instruments.

College Night

A joint college night sponsored by all the schools in the county can be both a service to the students and a possible fund raiser. If the colleges are charged a small fee for presenting and if a dinner is provided, the counselors can raise money for scholarships for needy and deserving students. It is also good public relations for the department when they can present a scholarship to a student at the awards night program.

Skill 19.3 Evaluating and Identifying Educational and Vocational Materials

Appropriate materials are instrumental in helping students make education decisions in relation to their career goals. Finding good materials is part of the school counselor's task. Guidelines for the preparation and evaluation of career and occupational literature have been formulated by the *National Career Development Association* (NCDA). These guidelines are appropriate for use in all vocational and education materials for both publishers and users. They also serve as the basis for ratings of career and occupational literature by the *Career Information Review Service* of NCDA in the *Career Development Quarterly*.

General areas of evaluation should include:

1. *Dates of publication* in order to determine if the material is current. Material over five years old should be discarded as new information is usually available.

2. A*ccuracy of information* which is free from distortion and advertising. The material should be reviewed by trained experts in the evaluation process and reflect different points of view. Data should be based upon current and reliable research.

3. The *format* should be clear, concise and interesting.

4. The *vocabulary* should be appropriate to the age and level of the target group. Age ranges should be defined in presenting the material. Material targeted for young high school students, for example, should reflect appropriate language and style. The use of nonsexist language is important.

5. The *purpose of the information* should be presented in the introduction to the material and the target population should be clearly indicated.

6. *Bias and stereotyping* of individuals with a disability, or based upon gender, race, social status, ethnicity, age or religion should be carefully reviewed and deleted. Vocabulary should be gender-free and persons of both sexes should be portrayed equally.

7. The use of *graphics* is valuable but should be presented in a manner that is accurate, current, and unbiased as to sex, race, age and physical disabilities.

The content of all career materials should:

1. Describe the *duties and nature of the work* in a clear and interesting fashion. Literature describing the field should include the importance of the occupation in a global sense; the availability of the occupations; the skills, knowledge and abilities of members in the field; the different levels of occupations in the field; and the nature of any specializations.

2. Portray the *work setting and conditions* of the work environment in terms of the physical and mental duties of the work, the hours, required travel and any aspects of the work that might be considered undesirable.

3. Include the *preparation required* for entrance into the occupation, together with the training, knowledge, skills, and abilities of those successful in the occupation. The levels of preparation in each level of the occupation should also be described.

4. Delineate *special requirements or considerations* needed for employment in the occupation. These include bona fide physical requirements, licensing, and certification or membership requirements. Social and psychological factors that impact on one's lifestyle should also be addressed.

5. Describe a variety of *methods of entry* into the occupation.

6. Include information about *earnings and benefits*.

7. Portray *advancement possibilities* and the criteria for such advancement.

8. Address the long term *employment outlook*. This is an important part of the evaluation.

9. Include *opportunities for experience and exploration* to ascertain if that field is appropriate for a specific individual.

10. Describe *related occupations* that share similar requirements.

11. Offer *additional sources of information*.

The National Career Development Association publishes a Career and Occupational Literature Reviewer's Rating Form that is available from NCDA, 5999 Stevenson Avenue, Alexandria, Va. 20034. This form can be used by guidance departments to rate material that is being considered for purchase for the guidance department or the library.

Finding Appropriate Materials

It is the job of the counselor to be able to readily access useful information as needed for different students and varying needs. Becoming familiar with available references can help, followed by regular monitoring of new information. Career and occupational materials change quickly due to frequent shifts in the world of work and technological advances, so the school counselor must stay abreast of current materials.

Federal Government Sources

O*NET, a website run by the U.S. Department of Labor that provides helpful information about career trends to users at no cost. This site can be accessed through the Department of Labor's website for Education and Training Administration at www.doleta.gov/. Other sites and useful documents can be accessed here as well.

This is a list of useful resources from the federal government.

1. Employment & Training Administration, Department of Labor, *Dictionary of Occupational Titles (DOT)* - A comprehensive source of information about occupations and characteristics of the workers in individual occupations.

2. Employment & Training Administration, Department of Labor, *Selected Characteristics of Occupations Defined in the Dictionary of Occupational Titles.*

3. Employment & Training Administration, Department of Labor, *Guide for Occupational Exploration.*

4. Bureau of Labor Statistics, Department of Labor, *Occupational Outlook Handbook.* (Available online at www.bls.gov/oco/; updated every two years.)

5. Bureau of Labor Statistics, Department of Labor, *Occupational Outlook Quarterly.* (Available online at www.bls.gov/opub/ooq/ooqhome.htm.)

6. Department of Defense, *Military Career Guide.*

7. Office of Federal Statistical Policy & Standards, Department of Commerce, *Standard Occupational Classification Manual.*

8. Office of Management & Budget, Executive Office of the President, *Standard Industrial Classification Manual.*

9. National Center for Education Statistics, Department of Education, *A Classification of Industrial Programs.*

10. Bureau of the Census, Department of Commerce, *U.S. Census of Population 1990, Classified Index of Industries and Occupations.*

Other Governmental Sources

Regional sources include the *Bureau of Labor Statistics* regional centers. The Michigan State Department of Education notes many resources and useful information at www.michigan.gov/mde/0,1607,7-140-6530_2629---,00.html.

Local sources include the chamber of commerce, the employment and rehabilitative services offices, community colleges and four year institutions, the private industry council, and civic or service organizations.

Commercial Sources of Information

There are many publishers who specialize in providing information about careers and vocations. Always evaluate their products using the guidelines noted above before utilizing these materials. Also be aware of the intent of the source, such as selling a particular product or program.

COMPETENCY 20.0 Understand career assessment and career decision-making programs

Skill 20.1 Decision Making and Career Development

The process of decision making is used in all stages of career development. Although decision making in career development is a continuous process there are critical points that occur in the selection of an entry level job, a change of job or a change in educational plans.

H.B. Gelatt in 1962 advocated "a totally rational approach to making decisions." Since then, he has changed his view of decision making to being flexible, keeping an open mind, and using one's intuition. His definition of decision making is "the process of arranging and rearranging information into a course of action."

The three parts of Gelatt's decision making process are as follows:

1. Obtain the information that forms the basis for making the decision. All information can be biased by the fact that it is ever-changing and slanted by the sender of the information.

2. Arrange and rearrange this information by being flexible and having knowledge of your individual needs.

3. Make a choice. Try to be rational but if the decision seems irrational have a good reason for making that decision.

Tiedman and **O'Hara** have noted that career choices are made by decision making processes that are subjective and depend upon the comprehension and control of the person making the decision. Their model tries to make the individual aware of all the factors involved in making the decision so they can make choices based on knowledge of themselves and of all the external factors involved.

They describe a process of decision making that is divided into two phases. The first is the anticipation phase and the second is the accommodation phase. Each has several steps.

Anticipation Phase

In the *exploration stage* the individual investigates all educational, occupational and personal alternatives. They identify interests and capabilities and consider the relationships among them and the alternatives suggested. The counselor provides support and teaching experiences as to the method of exploration and also provides career information.

In the *crystallization stage* the individual organizes, evaluates, synthesizes and orders the personal information and the alternatives from the exploration stage. Ideas are stabilized and formed as to possible career choices. The counselor helps in the organization, evaluation and synthesis of the information. Free discussion of issues and options continue to take place.

In the *choice stage* the individual makes a choice based upon the information gained in the crystallization stage with the consequences of the choice made as part of the process.

In the *clarification stage* the individual forms and carries out a plan to implement their choice. The counselor continues to supply information, support and feedback about the implementation of the choice.

Accommodation Phase

In the *induction stage,* usually during the first months of the implementation of the choice, individuals come to understand the reality of the choice they have made. They begin to learn what is expected and required of them.

In the *reformation stage* individuals work out the realities of the choices they have made, become more comfortable with those choices and begin to rely less on the support and advice of the counselor.

In the *integration stage* of the decision making process, individuals integrate their identities with those in the choice setting and experience a sense of equilibrium.

Because decision making is a product of personality and values, it is important for the individual to have experiences that contribute to their emotional maturity, self-concept and values. Counselors should be the providers of information and resources about the use of that information so that an intelligent choice can be made. The counselor should also help individuals improve upon and perhaps learn different decision making strategies. Ultimately, once the necessary tools and resources are obtained, the decision is the responsibility of the individual.

Skill 20.2 Student Appraisal Data Relevant to Career Development

Career development is a continuing process. It involves the evaluation of assessment results throughout the life span of an individual. Reflecting this concept, career counseling has grown from a trait-factor, counselor-dominated process to a developmental, client-centered process. This approach views assessment as a tool to increase self-awareness at every major transition period of the individual.

Objectives at each level of development enhance the growth of the individual, with one tool being the assessment instrument. The role of assessment in career development counseling has been recognized as important by the National Occupation Information Coordinating Committee (a federal interagency program) by establishing national guidelines for student and adult career development competencies. Go to www.ed.gov/pubs/TeachersGuide/noicc.html for more information and resources.

At the *elementary school* level, a career development objective might be increased self-awareness in relation to the world of work. This would entail the identification of personal interests, abilities, strengths and weaknesses as well as learning to value the benefits of education. Students could describe school activities that might help them be successful on a job as well as identifying academic skills needed in specific occupations of interest to the student.

At the *middle school* level, a career development objective might be to measure student preferences in different areas and their influence on the student's positive self-concept. This would entail that the student describe their personal likes and dislikes and to know of the benefits of education to career opportunities. The student should learn about his/her strengths and weaknesses in school subjects, what requirements and skills are needed for present and future occupations, the importance of academic and occupational skills in the working world, and the relationship of aptitudes and abilities to occupational groups.

At the *high school* level, it is important for the student to understand the relationship between educational success and work requirements, the role a positive self-concept plays in the world of work, and how individual characteristics relate to achieving life goals. At this level the student should be able to describe the relationship between academic and vocational skills to their own personal interests, ability and skills as well as how they can apply their own skills to present and future occupational needs.

Vernon Zunker, with influence from other theorists, has established a model for the use of assessment results in developmental career counseling. He describes four major steps: analyzing needs, establishing the purpose of testing, determining the instruments to be used, and utilizing the results in decision making for training and education.

The four steps for using assessment results in career counseling are:

Analyze needs - A needs analysis should be conducted using biographical data, interviews, and educational and work records. The cooperation and participation of the individual in establishing their needs is important for the success of the results. To assist the counselor in identifying needs a *counseling relationship must be established* to help the student articulate his/her needs. The *acceptance and adoption of the student's views* will enhance the relationship as well as help in exploring their views in relation to realistic career goals. The *lifestyle needs* of the individual should be part of the needs assessment in order to relate the world of work to the student's values, recreational requirements, financial needs, family responsibilities and societal obligations. The *specific needs* of the individual for assessment should then be examined. A decision should be made as to the need for an assessment instrument.

Establish the purpose of testing - After the needs analysis is completed the counselor and student should decide the purpose of testing. Testing can be used for diagnosis, prediction and comparison of individuals with a normed group. Testing does not always meet all needs that have been identified. The purpose of testing can be specific, as in predicting success in an education or training program, or more general, as in establishing an overall direction of career exploration. The counselor should explain the purpose of each test to be administered as well as the desired results in relation to the stated needs.

Determine the instruments to be used - Tests to be used for career assessment should measure ability, achievement, career maturity, interests, personality and values. Achievement tests measure academic strengths and weaknesses. Career maturity inventories measure vocational development in reference to self-awareness, planning and decision making abilities. Interest tests compare the individual's interests with reference groups. Personality and value inventories reflect traits that influence behavior. Any of the test results can stimulate interaction between the counselor and the student about the relationship between work satisfaction and the actual work.

Utilize the results - The counselor and the student use the results of the assessments to discuss the unique individual characteristics of the student and their relation to career exploration. The test results are also used to help students view themselves as a whole person. Individual traits and characteristics are used to determine plans for the present and to look into the changing future.

COMPETENCY 21.0 Understand postsecondary education planning

Skill 21.1 Postsecondary Education Options

Many students pursue further education once they receive their high school diploma. A significant part of the high school counselor's work involves helping students apply for admission to colleges and universities, as well as other education and training programs. A number of students will want to enroll in a college course of study that leads to a bachelor's degree. There are many resources available (as noted elsewhere in this guide) to help students identify possible schools of interest, including on-site visits from college admissions counselors. The application process is one counselor should be familiar with, and support students as they fill out forms, write essays and gather needed credentials and materials. For some programs, the process is quite involved.

Educational and Vocational Training Opportunities

There are many opportunities for students to obtain work training and education besides the pursuit of a bachelor's degree. Often these other paths lead to higher paying positions in areas that are wide open for employment due to a lack of trained personnel in these areas. Some of these options follow.

1. *Vocational Education* - Often offered by public or regional area vocational centers in daytime, evening and weekend classes. These classes range from basic entry level programs to advanced classes to help students develop a variety of skills in fields such as computers, electricity and plumbing. If a student is of high school age the program is usually part of the high school curriculum. If the individual is of adult age the cost is usually low or there is an opportunity to obtain financial aid. See www.directoryofschools.com/North-American-Trade-Schools/Home.htm for more information.

2. *Community Colleges, Junior Colleges, & Vocational -Technical Colleges* - Most of these schools admit students who might not have the qualifications to enter a four year institution. This gives the student who is a late bloomer or has not done well in high school a second chance. Classes are scheduled so that individuals who may be holding full-time jobs can attend. The cost is usually reasonable and financial aid is available. The completion of these programs can lead to an associate degree, a certificate, a job promotion, or a new career.

3. *Private Career/Proprietary Schools* - These for-profit schools offer training in specific skill areas. They usually are more expensive than a public institution but have placement facilities. Financial aid is usually available. They are accredited by state and/or national groups. A guide to choosing a private career school is Myers and Scott's *Getting Skilled, Getting Ahead*.

4. *Apprenticeship Programs* - These are usually administered through a labor-union industrial council. Forty to fifty occupations are represented by classroom instruction and on-the-job training. The programs involve from two to six years. Contacts for apprenticeship programs can usually be made through the state employment office.

5. *On-the-Job Training*- These programs are similar to apprenticeship programs but are of shorter length and are usually part of a job orientation program for new employees.

6. *The Job Training Partnership Act (JTPA)* - This is an adult training or retraining program funded by the government and run by a local private industry council (PIC) in localities where there is a need for employment training in the area.

7. *Health Related Training* - This type of training is usually available at hospitals or hospital-related institutions where there is an opportunity for clinical or field study as part of the formal instruction.

8. *Military Service* - The military services offer training and continued training in fields that can be used after the individual leaves the service. The Reserve Officers' Training Corps (ROTC) program offers students the opportunity to receive up to a full scholarship for four years of study in exchange for an extended time in the military.

Skill 21.2 Locating and Securing Scholarship and Financial Aid Assistance

The guidance department should have a collection of books and information to help students locate and secure scholarships and financial aid. There are printed guides available, although many students and parent/guardian(s) find using the internet most helpful.

There are many resources online. Although some commercial sites may provide useful information, they may not be the best or most unbiased sources, and some charge a fee. Two free non-commercial sites with good information are www.finaid.org and www.studentaid.ed.gov. Most colleges and technical schools also provide detailed information about financial aid on their individual websites.

Searching for specific scholarships should not be ignored. The class of the student (such as race, gender, or sexual orientation), area of study, membership in certain organizations and other elements can lead to **specialized financial aid** options. An example of a resource in this arena is "The Higher Education Money Book for Women and Minorities" published by Young, Mathews & Cox.

A great resource for counselors is the financial aid workshops offered by many colleges and universities to interested high schools free of charge. It is the counselor's job to organize and advertise the workshop which is provided by college staff members who are experts in financial aid. Sponsoring a **Financial Aid Night** is an excellent way for students and parent/guardian(s) to gain useful information about aid options and build relationships with the counselors. It is also another chance for the school to promote the guidance program.

Local public and college libraries can be good sources of information as well. Further, it is important that the counselor attends workshops explaining the new regulations involving federal money sources such as the *Pell Grant* and other federal funding sources for educational loans.

Subarea: GUIDANCE PROGRAMS AND PROFESSIONAL KNOWLEDGE

COMPETENCY 22.0 Apply procedures for determining and reporting comprehensive guidance and counseling program needs, priorities, and objectives

Skill 22.1 Needs Assessment and Program Evaluation Techniques

Needs Assessment - The needs assessment is an extensive preliminary study of the real and perceived wants and requirements of a population, community or group. A series of complete and extensive questions are formulated to be submitted to all facets of the population involved. The design of the needs assessment study should be carefully formulated so the results can be analyzed in relation to the purpose of the study.

For example, a needs assessment of a school community would consist of community taxpayers, community leaders, parents, school administrators, teachers, support staff and students. Other individuals may come forward who wish to participate in the study and they should be included if they have a connection with the purpose of the study.

Program Evaluation Techniques - Program evaluation is often a requirement of funding sources or of administrators. Some there is a sincere wish to see if a program is producing the desired results; other times the demand for an evaluation is the result of political pressure, to either discredit opponents of the program or to strengthen their own positions on the value of the program. Finances influence the requirement of a program evaluation for a variety of reasons.

There are two broad types of program evaluation: formative and summative.

Formative Evaluation - This type of evaluation involves the collection of data while a program is in the *developmental, implementational,* or *operational* stage. In the *developmental* stage the evaluator tries to determine the general goals, the specific outcomes or behaviors to be attained, and the current performance level of the population of the program to be evaluated. In the *implementational* stage the evaluator tries to determine if the program is implemented appropriately and the identified population is participating in the program. In the *operational* stage the evaluator looks at how well the program is running. Other information to gather is finding out if the staff is adequate and well trained and if any unanticipated difficulties have surfaced.

Summative Evaluation - This type of evaluation involves the collection of data after a program has been in place for a period of time. The summative evaluation is often done after one year of operation. This may not be an adequate amount of time to determine the effectiveness of the program, depending on the nature of the program. The summative evaluation often is used to determine if the program will be continued.

Models used in evaluation can be classified in the following manner.

The **CIPP Model** has four stages. *Context evaluation* identifies the elements of a setting and the discrepancies between what exists and what is desirable. *Input evaluation* is the analysis of available resources and methods for the selection of the most appropriate course of action. *Process evaluation* is the collection of data about the progress of the program. *Product evaluation* is the process of determining the extent to which the program has achieved its goals. In this model the evaluator gathers the information needed to make a decision in each stage and presents this material to the administrator for decision making.

Discrepancy Evaluation - The evaluator compares the degree of agreement between program standards and program performance. *Program standards* are the criteria the developers of the program identified for utilization of resources, procedural operations, program management and final outcomes. *Program performance* is what actually occurred when the program was operational in the educational setting. The five questions the evaluator answers are:

    Are standards defined in measurable terms?
    Are behavioral objectives stated clearly?
    What instruments are developed or selected to measure the standards?
    What data has been collected on performance?
    Has the data been used to determine the discrepancy between standards and performance?

The findings of the evaluator are then submitted in a report.

Adversarial Evaluation - The evaluator and administrator, with the help of the personnel involved in the program, compile a list of issues to evaluate. Issues are selected that are determined to be the most important to the success of the program. Selected personnel form teams to either support or oppose the program, gathering information to support their stand and prepare arguments for their side of the issues. The teams present their arguments before a panel of decision makers who make the final decision as to the modification, elimination or retention of the program.

Skill 22.2 Developing Objectives and Determining Outcomes Based on Data

All programs in the guidance curriculum need to be based on clear objectives and evaluated effectively. New and innovative programs and methods are sometimes introduced without careful consideration of their value for the setting in which they are to be used. The school counselor should assess new programs before implementing them.

Factors to consider are:
- Will this program be acceptable to the community?
- What will be the cost to the school district?
- Can grant money be obtained to initiate the program?
- Will that money be available on a continuous basis or will it run out after a period of time?

A needs assessment of the school community might be in order to see if the program is acceptable. As an example, the health department might feel a program of smoking cessation would be beneficial to the students. In a needs assessment survey, students might feel that smoking is a desired activity on their part and so they would not attend this type of activity. It might be more advantageous to the health department to develop a unit on the health damage smoking causes to the individual in later life.

Before adding a program to the guidance and counseling curriculum, how this task will be accomplished should be evaluated. Will new staff be needed or will this program fall to the existing staff? If the latter is the case, will other programs now in existence have less time allotted or can some ineffective program now be eliminated? Can the staff view the suggested new program in operation in another school? If this can be done, the counselors in the other school should be questioned as to the strengths and weaknesses of the program, how they would change the program, and what benefits have the students experienced by instituting this program.

Program objectives should be developed before the adoption of any program. These objectives are based upon the needs of the population to be served and can be drawn from the needs assessment. Program objectives should be written with measurable goals and a clear methodology for evaluating the achievement or lack of achievement of the goals.

After all evaluative data have been compiled and analyzed, the person in charge of the program determines the degree to which program objectives have been obtained. If the formulation of the program objectives was done carefully and there is indisputable evidence that these objectives have not been reached, it is ethical to eliminate the program and start again from scratch. If there is an undeniable opinion that the program objectives have been obtained, then the retention of the program and further plans for expansion should be the result.

Problems can arise when there is no clear evidence of attainment of program objectives, or if some of the objectives have been attained but others, considered more important, have not been accomplished. It is clear that modification of the program is in order. The task of rebuilding the methods in order to reach the stated objectives should begin with a new perspective of what needs to be done to improve the program. Perhaps people who have not had initial input into the program should be recruited to help in the revision of the program. Perhaps the original objectives of the program were unrealistic. These can be difficult questions to resolve and require thought and effort.

COMPETENCY 23.0 Apply knowledge of professional responsibilities, standards, and issues related to school counselors

Skill 23.1 Professional Standards of the American School Counseling Association (ASCA) and American Counseling Association (ACA)

In the past, divisions of ACA, such as ASCA, had their own code of ethics, but in 1997, with the revision of the code, divisions were asked to dissolve their codes and develop Best Practice Guidelines as a basic coverage with specific codes that apply to their specialty areas. To review ASCA standards, go to www.schoolcounselor.org/content.asp?contentid=173.

The ACA Code of Ethics and Standards of Practice were first developed in 1961 and revised in 1974. Since then they were revised approximately every seven years, the latest revision being in 2005. These codes are detailed below.

The Counseling Relationship
The relationship between counselors and clients is based on trust and respect. Therefore, counselor is responsible for respecting the dignity of all clients and always being mindful of the clients' welfare. The counselor must keep appropriate records, get informed consent, maintain professional boundaries, be culturally and developmentally competent, and be ever vigilant about avoiding harm to clients.

Confidentiality
It is important the counselors provide their services in a culturally competence manner that respects the rights of the client. Clients must be provided with information and guidelines by which the counselor may breech confidentiality. This informed consent may need to be reviewed throughout the counseling relationship. Records containing sensitive information about clients should be handled with the great care and discretion in location. Exceptions of confidentiality may include when clients are in danger of harming themselves or someone else and when the counselor's work with the client is court-ordered, with disclosure being a condition of the counseling. At all times, the counselor must make every effort to protect the information the client has disclosed within the confines of the trust-based relationship.

Professional Responsibility
Counselors must have a working knowledge of their ethical responsibilities as they work with clients. To best serve their clients, counselors need to know the extent of their competence (knowing when to refer a client to another provider), be involved with continued professional development, clearly and realistically publicize their services, fairly represent their professional qualifications, monitor the effectiveness of services rendered, and rigorously practice codes of conduct that are nondiscriminatory.

Relationships with other Professionals
Consultation is a powerful tool in the counseling practice. No counselor is expected nor should be expected to know how to work with all populations, cases, and presenting challenges. Establishing relationships with other professionals and specialists allows counselors to discuss the effectiveness of case management, maintain confidentiality, and to increase overall effectiveness of the services provided to the client.

Evaluation, Assessment, and Interpretation
Assessments may be related to education, career or psychological issues. Intended use of any instrument must be disclosed to the client. Multicultural considerations are taken into account to avoid assessments that are inappropriate due to a biased empirical background. Part of counselors' continued professional development is to ensure that any assessment used is the most recent version available. Legal proceedings for forensic evaluations can include that of the professional opinion of the counselor as well as written or court-ordered consent.

Teaching, Training, and Supervision
Consultation with professionals allows supervising counselors to ethically monitor the work of counselors-in-training. Before serving as a supervisor, counselors undergo extensive training in policy and procedures in the areas of appraisal and evaluation. Supervisors have an ethical obligation to the clients of the supervisee to ensure the services provided are appropriate. Supervisors need to encourage counselors-in-training to refrain from providing counseling and related services when their physical, mental and emotional well-being are called in to question.

Research and Publications
It is imperative that counselors establish and maintain ethical standards in conducting research. Participants must be notified of the purpose of the study, and how their input or results will be used, as well as receive information about the results of the overall project. Federal and state laws as well as institutional regulations need to be firmly adhered to.

Resolving Ethical Issues
Following ethical and professional standards is critical to the importance of the work counselors do with their clients. Ethical standards not only prevent harm to the client, but also protect the counselor from making unfounded and unintentional mistakes. Counselors need to consult with other counseling professionals about any situation or case that warrants an ethical question or decision. Should a counselor suspect a colleague of ethical misconduct, ACA expects counselors to follow the protocol as illustrated in the ACA Policy and Procedures for Processing Complaints of Ethical Violations.

These eight topics cover the most often questioned areas of ethical practice. They are by no means all inclusive; instead they are guidelines as to basic ethical behavior. Although the ethics guidelines are more specific than standards of practice, they cannot possibly include all situations. Standards of practice are, by their nature, more generic and provide basic behavior standards for all counselors. These codes serve the purpose of identifying areas of concern, not of providing a "cook book recipe" as to standards of conduct or as to the resolution of specific ethical situations.

When an issue of ethics arises in the counselor's practice in any context (i.e., private practice, a school setting or an agency) it is wise to have one's own process of determining the course of action. Reference to the ACA Code of Ethics would be the first step in the resolution of the problem. Additionally, after formulating a course of action, all the ramifications of that course of action should be weighed. If there are any doubts as to the ethics of this course of action, colleagues, attorneys and specialists should be consulted.

To view ACA's Code of Ethics or access resources related to ethical dilemmas, go to www.counseling.org/Resources/CodeOfEthics/TP/Home/CT2.aspx.

Skill 23.2   Professional Development

Licensure and Certification

Professional counselors can be certified in different areas (such as school counseling) by the National Board of Certified Counselors (NBCC) (www.nbcc.org), as well as licensed by many states. These certifying agents have their own codes of ethics to which members are accountable. The counselor who holds each specific certification or license is ethically bound and accountable to know and abide by their ethical code. Violations can and should be reported to these monitoring agencies for potential consequences to the counselor.

Continuing Education and Professional Connections

All licensing and certifying bodies require a requisite number of hours of continuing education per year or certification period. Regardless, all school counselors have a professional and ethical responsibility to stay abreast of current developments in the field. Continuing education opportunities can also provide useful support and connections with other professionals in the field.

Attending conferences and seminars can be professionally nourishing, and helpful in preventing burnout in what can be a very demanding career. In addition to going to programs geared specifically to school counseling and guidance, counselors may find it interesting and helpful to participate in workshops and training programs designed for mental health professionals, educators, social workers, and administrators. Attending meetings of the local, state and national counselor associations can also be informative.

There are two professional associations for school counselors in Michigan. The Michigan School Counselors Association can be reached at www.mich-sca.org, and the Association of Michigan School Counselors' site is www.michiganschoolcounseling.org. Also, at the national level you can go to www.schoolcounselor.org/content.asp?pl=325&sl=129&contentid=129 for more information about professional development opportunities.

COMPETENCY 24.0 Understand the structure and functions of the Michigan Comprehensive Guidance and Counseling Program

Skill 24.1 Michigan's Comprehensive Guidance and Counseling Program

The state of Michigan's Department of Education has outlined a Comprehensive Guidance and Counseling Program "to assist students in identifying, planning, and attaining those goals consistent with their aptitudes, needs, abilities, and interests." The intent is to provide coordinated and effective guidance and counseling services for all students, K-12 and beyond.

Program Components

The four components of the program are identified as Guidance Curriculum, Individual Planning, Responsive Services, and Systems Support.

The **Guidance Curriculum** refers to organized, planned experiences throughout the school years to teach students in three content areas: Career Knowledge and Exploration, Knowledge of Self and Others, and Educational/Career-Technical Development.

Individual Planning consists of a range of activities in which students are assisted in laying a course of learning and action to help them achieve their academic, personal and career goals.

Responsive Services include personal counseling, collaboration with parents and others, as well as referrals to meet immediate needs.

Systems Support involves management activities that support the guidance program including planning, professional development and community relations.

The Standard

The state standard is that each school district is to adopt a customized version of the Comprehensive Guidance and Counseling Program. The benchmarks of the program include the following:

1. An action plan to ensure that services and programs are in place;

2. A mission statement that is consistent with the goals of the school district;

3. The use of a needs assessment to best meet the needs of the community and the school district;

4. The provision of programs to ensure student competency in the content areas noted above in the Guidance Curriculum

5. All four components of the Comprehensive Guidance and Counseling Program as listed above (Guidance Curriculum, Individual Planning, Responsive Services, and Systems Support);

6. A developmentally-targeted program provided to all students K-12; and

7. Appropriate evaluation measures to ensure ongoing improvement and revision.

The details of this program can be reviewed at www.michigan.gov/mde/0,1607,7-140-6530_2629_2722---,00.html. A range of related resources are also available at and through this website.

TEACHER CERTIFICATION STUDY GUIDE

COMPETENCY 25.0   Apply consultation, collaboration, and coordination procedures

Skill 25.1 Components of a Consultation Model

The purpose of all consultation procedures is to problem-solve. The principals in the consultation process are the consultant, usually the counselor in a school setting, but could also be a person knowledgeable in the problem at hand, and the consultee, often a teacher or other school personnel. The consultee is not usually the student whose problem is the topic of discussion. Although the student has a vital part in the process, the purpose of the consultation is to aid the consultee in solving a problem that usually concerns a student or a group of students. In the school setting, consultees can be one or more school personnel, and consultants can be more than one person with knowledge of the student and/or expertise in the solving of this particular problem.

Most often the consultation process is used to solve an academic problem of a student. However, school problems increasingly involve difficulties of a societal nature that affect the school environment and school population as a whole. School policy issues are often solved by employing the consultation model. Some examples of these issues are dress codes, drug policies, and issues of sudden death in the school community. Different approaches are used depending upon the particular goal of the consultant and consultee.

The consultant can take the role of an **advocate** in directly presenting evidence and attempting to persuade the consultee to take some stand or action. The advocacy can be in support of a student, a group of students or an idea to be implemented.

The consultant can also act in the capacity of an **expert** in a particular field. This role is employed when there is a need to inform or educate the consultee in a specialized area. For the school counselor this may take the form of interpretation of test data, psychological and environmental background information, or placement data.

Another role of the consultant would entail specific **training and education** in an area such as identifying "children at risk." The goal here is to develop school-wide plans and procedures to improve the rate of drop outs, for example.

The counselor/consultant's role most often used in the school setting is that of **consultant/collaborator** where the consultee and the consultant's roles are equal in attempting to solve the problem. It is a three pronged relationship; the counselor/consultant, the teacher/consultee and the student and, at times, the student's parents). As a collaborator, the counselor takes part of the responsibility for implementing the plan to solve the problem. This may take on the role of directly working with the student to reinforce behavior change.

GUIDANCE COUNSELOR

The task of **fact finding** (gathering relevant information, studying it and disseminating it to the consultee) falls upon the shoulders of the consultant.

The other role the consultant can take is that of the **process specialist**, in which the counselor outlines the steps needed to reach mutual goals.

There is a common procedure for all consultation processes, although the settings in which the consultation takes place may differ. Some of these places are:

1. A clinical setting which can be a mental health facility.
2. A school setting with the parent, teacher or administrator present.
3. A training setting for education purposes.
4. A school or business with the staff of an organization.

Prior to the first session, the consultant should gather certain data. These include background information as to the purpose of the consultation process, some of the political considerations of the process (when applicable), and other facts that may help the consultant in understand the dynamics of the situation.

The goals of the consultation should be formulated so that all concerned parties know where the process is headed. The function, role, techniques and procedures used by the consultant in the consultation process should be formulated after the above issues are determined.

The experience of the consultee in the consultation process should be taken into consideration so that if additional education and skill training are required the consultant is prepared to furnish that training.

Some of the common procedures for all consultation processes are as follows:

A. Entry and Relationship Building

Consulting in the school setting most involves an attempt to change student behavior. For success, the process must obtain the trust and confidence of the student and to motivate the student to change. Further, the student needs to be willing to cooperate in the plans for implementing behavior change. Once the student is on board, the consultant can then proceed in implementing the process of consultation by contacting other parties involved, such as the child's parents, teachers, experts in areas of special needs and any other support personnel deemed important in solving the problem. As far as possible, the student should be included in defining the problem with the consultee, especially at the secondary level, and should also be included in meetings during which the strategies to be used are developed.

B. Diagnosis and Definition of Problem

It should be clear to all participants what has been diagnosed as the problem. Quite often the consultee and the student see the problem in different lights and therefore a plan to solve the problem cannot work if the student and consultee are at odds. In a situation where a student needs to modify behavior, the model of **behavior consultation**, based on the theory of social learning, is employed. Specific changes in behavior are sought. Information regarding the problem is obtained; the problem is defined in detail; goals are set; plan strategies are developed; assessment criteria are agreed upon; and avenues of intervention are explored. Solving the problem depends upon the consultee "making it happen"; therefore, it is critical that the consultee has ownership of the plan.

Other models of consultation are **organization consultation** where the problem is in the organizational framework. This is most often used when an expert in that particular area is required. The **doctor/patient** model is when an organization knows there is a problem but does not know the nature of the problem. When the interactions of the members of an organization are examined, **process consultation** is employed. When the mental health of a community can be improved by consulting with other human services professionals in the delivery of their services, **mental health consultation** is employed.

C. Devising and Implementing a Plan

In devising a plan, the counselor/consultant, together with the student and the consultee (teacher), identify a behavior that is of most concern to all. A plan of action is devised as to how to expedite change with equal input from all participants involved. Techniques of encouragement, logical consequences, praise and reward are used to reach goals set down by all parties. The consultant needs to monitor the process and identify problems with the implementation so the plan can be changed if necessary.

D. Evaluation and Summarization

Although the initial meeting is usually not the only meeting, a summary of what has transpired during the meeting should be made before terminating the session. Each participant should fully understand their role in implementing behavior change and should be held responsible for his/her part in the process. Once the behavior change has been accomplished, an evaluation of the process should be made by the consultant.

Skill 25.2 Strategies for Effective Collaboration

Assist Participants in Problem Solving

The counselor/consultant should have a plan of action to assist the participants in doing their parts in effecting change. This can take the role of teaching specific skills, as in the case of a teacher with no prior experience in attempting behavior change, or in helping the teacher devise strategies and sequential plans to deal with the defined behavior problem. The consultant should be able to help the consultee describe in detail the specific types of behavior that are problematic. If necessary, the consultant should make arrangements for any clerical help needed in order to relieve the teacher/consultee of this task.

Help should also be provided to the student and his/her parents in order for the consultation to affect the desired change in behavior. This should take the form of frequent contact to evaluate the progress of the process and to ascertain if more aid is needed or additional concerns on the part of the student and parent have arisen.

Communicate the Needs of the Student

It is important for the consultant not to assume what the needs of the student are without first clarifying those needs directly with the student. In the case of an adolescent, if this is not done first, trust will not be attained and the whole process is likely to fail. Permission to share these needs should be obtained from the student in order to reinforce the trust relationship.

Once this is done, a meeting should be held with the consultee to communicate these needs. If the student can be present, misunderstandings are less likely to occur. Such a meeting can also be a method to open lines of further dialogue between the student and the consultee. In this scenario the consultant acts in part as the advocate of the student/client using expertise acquired from experience. It is important the consultant balance the needs of the student/client with those of the consultee/teacher in order to achieve maximum results.

Involve Parent/Guardian(s) in Consultation

Parent/guardian(s) are a vital part of the consultation process. Consultation works best when the parent/guardian(s) are involved in the consultation process from the beginning. Even in the case of non-cooperative parents the consultant must inform them every step of the way. Often the situation is complicated by divorced and separated families, issues of custody, and the alienation of the student from his family. The consultant, while respecting the parent/guardian(s)'s rights, must always keep in mind the primary goal of solving the student's problem. (See Skill 26.1 for more information about involving parent/guardian(s) in the consultation process.)

Assist in the Use of Data and Resources

The consultant needs to have as much information about the situation and the student as possible. Do not rush into the consultation process without doing an adequate job of gathering data. Some of the things the consultant can do are:

1. Examine the permanent record for standardized test scores, patterns of grade fluctuation, weak and strong areas, and attendance record.

2. Talk with the present teacher(s) to ascertain if they are all having the same problem, and if not, gather insights from the teacher who is not having a problem.

3. Observe the student in the classroom, if possible.

4. Administer additional tests if necessary.

5. Gather medical, physical and discipline history.

Once you have some kind of analysis of the possible problem, compile a list of resources that might be available, both in and outside the school community, to be used as support mechanisms. This list may include:

- short or long term personal counseling, both for the student and the family
- alcohol and other drug counseling
- academic tutoring
- referral to the school psychologist for special education testing
- school social worker intervention for family visits and ongoing support

This list should be available when the consultation process begins, so if needed, action can be taken at that time.

Identify Procedures for Transition and Follow-Up

When it has been determined that the consultation process has been successful in solving the problem, a formal evaluation of the process is in order. This can be accomplished by a number of methods. Individual interviews with all parties involved in the process can be conducted or a survey instrument used to determine if the consultee and the student/client have been satisfied with the process. Input concerning the areas they feel need to be continued or modified, the process for the continuation of the plan, and comments relating to the entire procedure should also be solicited.

The consultant becomes increasingly less active in the consultation process as part of the transition phase, agreeing to decrease and eliminate the need for intervention in a gradual way. As a final step, after the consultant has not been involved for a period of time, a follow-up interview should be conducted as to the effectiveness of the process. If there is a regression on the part of the student, it may be appropriate to reinstitute the consultation process or make further referrals.

TEACHER CERTIFICATION STUDY GUIDE

COMPETENCY 26.0 Understand principles and procedures for establishing and maintaining effective school-home relationships

Skill 26.1 Parents and Guardians as Partners

Understanding the Needs of Parent/Guardian(s)

Parents and legal guardians are the people with whom school counselors are most likely to interact. In fact, without the express consent of parents and guardians, counselors are not permitted to discuss the student with any other family members.

Having an understanding of what parents and guardians need can be helpful in developing and maintaining positive relationships with parents and guardians. The three basic things that parents need from school counselors are respect, validation and support, and information.

Respect
As noted previously (see Skill 1.15), respect is a key element in effective communication. Parents and guardians may or may not be respectful of school personnel. The parents' history with members of the school community, their own experiences as a student, the current stresses in their lives and their general approach to life may influence how they respond to school counselors. Nonetheless, it is essential that counselors act respectfully in all of their interactions with parents and guardians.

Respect is conveyed through word choice, voice tone, and content. Positive, inclusive statements express respect. Questions that invite collaboration also suggest respect. A lack of reactivity helps maintain respectful interactions. Counselors need to remember that some people respond to any contact by someone from their child's school with fear and/or anger. Being non-reactive to the parent's response will aid the counselor in communicating respect and concern, and helps avoid unnecessary conflict.

Validation and Support
Parents and guardians need validation and support from school counselors, especially when addressing difficult issues. Direct comments such as "I know you want the best for your child" and "I'm sure you are doing your best to help your child" can be useful. It also may be helpful to introduce a sensitive concern with "You probably know this, but I wanted to tell you…." This takes into account that the parent may be aware of what the counselor is going to disclose and communicates that the counselor believes that the parent is tuned into his or her child. While this may not always be the case, it is better to err in this direction.

In spite of any failings, parents and guardians are doing their best. From the counselor's perspective, parents may not be meeting the student's needs. They may even be abusive and neglectful. When necessary, the school counselor may have to directly confront a parent or guardian, or file an abuse report. However, most of the time, parents and guardians are doing the best they can. Support and validation may also aid them in positively changing their behavior.

Information

The third thing parents and guardians need is clear information. The counselor needs to be direct in communicating his or her concerns about the student. As noted, the parent may or may not be aware of what has come to the counselor's attention. Parent/guardians have the right and need to be informed. They also need to hear what the counselor and other school personnel are proposing as an action plan. This information needs to be conveyed in a non-judgmental way, without direct or implied criticism of the parent, even when the counselor is asking the parent to do something differently.

Consultation as the Model for Interacting with Parents and Guardian

A good way to approach working with parents and guardians of students is to think about it as consultation. Interactions with parents and guardians are a two-way street: the counselor has information and concerns to share with the parent or guardian, who also has information and concerns to share with the counselor. A collaborative mindset will aid in eliciting cooperation and engagement with parents, and ultimately leads to the best results for the student.

Parent/guardian(s) are a valuable source of information about the student. Issues of family background and medical history information can only be obtained from parents or those adults who have been privy to family interaction. Such data can be very helpful in generating solutions to the problems the student is encountering in the school setting.

Non-cooperative parents may have an "attitude" about how the school has "not done right by" their child. It is in the best interest of all to permit them to vent their feelings. This may be one of the few times school personnel have listened to them. Emphasize that the school is not giving up on the child, and if in the past strategies for improvement have not worked, new strategies will be developed.

When consulting with parent/guardians, focus on the issue at hand as soon as possible after allowing them to vent. Explain the concerns and the tentative plan to the parents. Enlist the equal cooperation of parents by asking how they feel about the suggested course of action. Accept ideas for modification when appropriate, and help them see that they are a vital part of making the plan work.

Good counselors maintain an openness to possible solutions, modifying action plans as new information is gathered from parents. This openness includes being alert to their own assumptions about what is best for the student and what remedies or support is needed. Such an approach will also communicate to parents their significance and value, further aiding true collaboration.

Be careful not to overwhelm parents and guardians by giving them too many tasks, keeping in mind they may have too much stress in their daily lives already. Encourage them to feel that you, collectively, are developing a workable plan that may need modifying as it progresses. It is important to set up checkpoints to contact them about the progress of the course of action. If additional contact is not made, the parents will be negative about the entire process and further intervention on the part of the school will be extremely difficult.

On a more general level, another avenue to engage parent/guardians as collaborators is to form a parent advisory committee. This group can serve as a resource to the guidance department and help create open channels of communication between school counselors and parent/guardian(s).

Skill 26.2 Knowledge of Family Dynamics

Families of students may consist of a variety of people besides a mother, father and siblings. This is especially true of families who have experienced the disruption of divorce, death, homelessness, natural disasters, mental health and addiction problems and other issues. Being alert to the various configurations of "family" is crucial to effectively serving students and families. Similarly, sensitivity to and knowledge of different social-cultural groups as they relate to family structure is also important.

Awareness of the issues that particular families face as outlined in Skill 3.1 (Specific Populations) is also essential. The stresses on many families impair their abilities to support students adequately, and sensitivity on the part of school counselors to these issues can be useful. This awareness can help by avoiding stigma and further stress as well as serving to ameliorate the existing stress by providing support and resources.

While counselors often find they need to serve as an advocate for students with colleagues, parents, and care providers, school counselors also may need to advocate for parents and guardians at times. Thinking of oneself as an advocate for families as well as for individual students can be beneficial. This stance is useful both in fostering positive relationships with parents and guardians, but also in producing positive results for the student.

Contributions from the Field of Family Therapy

Family therapy is a branch of counseling that addresses the well-being of families. It developed in the 1950's as a way to help families make changes in their functioning. Although it is beyond the scope of the job of school counselors to work with families in a therapeutic context, the field of family therapy has some useful insights for school counselors. This information can help counselors better understand and interact with family members in their efforts to help students succeed in school and life.

Family therapists draw on various theories and counseling approaches, including group dynamics, systems theory, psychodynamic theory and therapy, Gestalt, cognitive-behavioral therapy, object relations, narrative therapy and solution-focused therapy. They may have a background in child development, social work or psychology. What they agree on is that the family is the primary group within which each person learns how to behave with others.

Specifically, family therapy suggests that an individual's behavior derives from and is maintained not only by early family and caregiver experiences but by current experiences with whomever he or she perceives as family. Other people's behavior helps keep an individual acting in certain ways. Further, these interactions are often repetitive and circular, reinforcing each other. Therefore, in some cases, interventions need to include family members so that an individual is able to make behavioral changes.

Another contribution from family therapy is the understanding that there are overt and covert roles and rules that guide behavior in families. Family members may or may not be consciously aware of these parameters, but their behavior is still affected by them. In rigid families, any deviation from these rules and roles can cause distress in other family members and in the system as a whole. This reactivity can keep family members, especially children, from changing their behavior, even in other settings.

How families manage conflict is often a characteristic that defines a particular family. Some families avoid conflict at all costs; others seem to thrive on patterns of conflict. Often, "problem" children or adolescents (known as "the identified patient" in family therapy jargon) serve to keep the parents from addressing underlying issues. This conflict focuses family concern away from a more painful problem, almost always one that is grounded in the adult relationship(s).

More information about family therapy can be located at these websites: www.familytherapyresources.net/, www.mayoclinic.com, and en.wikipedia.org/wiki/Family_therapy.

Skill 26.3 Conducting an Orientation Program to the School and Guidance Program

A major change in the life of a child is the transition from home to school. For the student entering school for the first time, as well as the transitions from elementary to middle school, and middle school to high school, a smooth and anxiety-reducing procedure can be extremely useful. While the attitude of the parent/guardian is important, the school people the child has first contact with sets the tone for the school experience. Therefore, it is important that the organizers of the first encounter recognize the needs of the child and address these fears and needs through a student orientation.

Careful planning is essential. A written procedure to eliminate the possibility of omitting details important to the success of the orientation helps. Details include:

1. Parents receive advance notification of the time, date, and place of the orientation. The notice should include a student handbook with the school regulations clearly spelled out as well as penalties for infractions of the school rules.

2. The meeting is set for the early evening and lasts no more than an hour and one half.

3. The agenda for the meeting is carefully delineated ahead of time and at the meeting.

4. The principal and other school administrators are introduced, and their role in the school community explained.

5. The Guidance Department introduces its staff members, and explains the functions and programs of the department, including the procedures for seeing a counselor.

6. There should be a question and answer period that is restricted in duration.

7. At the middle and high school levels, discuss scheduling and give all students copies of their schedules. Additional copies should be available on the first day for the students who have not brought their copy to school.

8. A tour of the facilities can be conducted by upper class students to help the new students familiarize themselves with the building and the rooms in which their classes will be held.

9. If possible, refreshments should be served, with parents, students, and staff mingling in an informal atmosphere.

COMPETENCY 27.0 Apply knowledge of legal and ethical issues related to the rights and responsibilities of students, parents and guardians, and school personnel

Skill 27.1 Legal Rights of Students and Parents Concerning Student Records and Assessment Data

School employees, on a need-to-know basis, may have access to student records. These individuals may include principals, assistant principals, school psychologists, school counselors, and special education professionals. Regardless of his or her position, each employee must maintain the confidentiality of student information.

In 1973, Congress passed a federal statute called FERPA to clarify the legal rights of students and parent/guardian(s) concerning access to student records. Also known as the "Buckley Amendment, FERPA stands for Family Educational Rights and Privacy Act (20 U.S.C. § 1232g; 34 CFR Part 99). (Go to nces.ed.gov/forum/FERPA_links.asp for more information about FERPA.)

Schools that receive funds from the federal government must comply with FERPA. The rights afforded by FERPA apply to parent/guardian(s) of students under the age of eighteen. Once a student turns eighteen, these rights are then transferred to the "eligible" student.

Under 34 CFR Part 99.7, FERPA states that parent/guardian(s) be notified on an annual basis about their rights to have access to or review their student's records. The following criteria must be included in the annual notification:

1. Parent/guardian(s) have the right to review their child's records
2. Parent/guardian(s) can advocate for changes to be made to the record should any information be incorrect.
3. Parent/guardian(s) can provide or withhold consent for the disclosure of personal information located with their child's record.
4. The way in which a parent/guardian can file a complaint with the Department of Education concerning a school or institution's failure to comply with FERPA.
5. Define which school officials that may have access to school records.

Schools may use a variety of ways to inform parents about their rights such as the school or community newspaper, bulletin boards, and student handbooks. Schools are not required to individually inform parents of their rights. Schools must procure parental consent to share student personal information. For example, a high school counselor must have a consent form on file before providing information to a college concerning a student's academic background.

All assessment data are considered student records and must be kept confidential. Legally and ethically, only the students and/or their parent/guardian(s) have the right to access unless they have specifically signed a waiver or requested that the information be shared with colleges, outside professionals, or other personnel such as attorneys.

A good resource for issues related to student privacy and confidentiality can be found at nces.ed.gov/pubs2006/stu_privacy/intro.asp.

Skill 27.2 Legislation Regarding Exceptional Students

Special education law is filled with abbreviations. In the following explanations the abbreviations are used instead of the actual names of the acts or authorities. The following is a list of these abbreviations for easy reference. (See www.ed.gov for more information.)

EDGAR - Education Department General Administrative Regulations

EAHCA - Education for all Handicapped Children Act

EHA - Education for the Handicapped Act

FAPE - Free Appropriate Public Education

IEP - Individualized Education Program

IFSP - Individualized Family Service Plan

IDEA - Individuals with Disabilities Act

ITDA - Infants and Toddlers with Disabilities Act

LEA - Local Education Authority

OCR - Office of Civil Rights (U.S. Department of Education).

OSERS - Office of Special Education and Rehabilitative Services (U.S. Department of Education)

OSEP - Office of Special Education Programs (U.S. Department of Education)

SEA - State Education Authority

In 1975 Congress signed into law the Individuals with Disabilities Education Act (IDEA), or Public Law 94-142, making local and state education entities responsible for providing children with disabilities a "free and appropriate public education." This act was a turning point in the education of children with disabilities providing that these children have a right to FAPE and also provided for procedural protections to insure that they received this FAPE. Subsequently Section 504 of the Rehabilitation Act of 1993 was enacted and also affected educational rights of children with disabilities.

There are overlapping provisions as well as differences between these laws with Section 504 being broad and general, including a wider range of discrimination while IDEA is more specific and detailed. Other Acts delineate the delivery procedures of education services to children with disabilities.

Brown vs. Board of Education and Mills vs. Board of Education were two important legal decisions that helped hasten the enactment of education protections for children with disabilities. Section 504 of the Rehabilitation Act of 1993 provided that "No otherwise qualified handicapped individual ... shall solely by reason of his handicap be excluded from participation, in, be denied the benefits of, or be subjected to discrimination under any program or activity receiving federal assistance." The subsequent amendments provided for payment of costs of attorney's fees and damages to parents if they proved successful in legal suits brought against educational institutions for not providing their children with a FAPE.

IDEA is a funding vehicle of the Federal Government for a SEA to provide a FAPE to all children with disabilities. In addition if a state opts to provide a FAPE for children ages three to five and eighteen to twenty one, it must, under IDEA, provide that opportunity for all children with disabilities in those age groups. In addition if any children without disabilities in those age groups are provided with educational services, then a proportionate share of those with disabilities must also be provided with that educational service. The funding is provided by a complicated formula taking into account the number of children in a given state who have been classified as disabled.

Each state monitors the devising and implementing its own FAPE. The main provision enacted by Congress was the requirement that each child classified be provided with an IEP on an annual basis. Procedural protections include that the child be identified, evaluated by a multi-disciplinary team, eligibility for special education determined, and an IEP developed with parental participation.

TEACHER CERTIFICATION STUDY GUIDE

Skill 27.3 Laws Regarding Child Abuse and Neglect

Every state has laws that require the reporting of suspected abuse and neglect of children under the age of 18 (see Michigan law below). The school counselor should review state law as well as the policies of the school district in order to become familiar with the definitions of abuse, the mandate to report, and the procedures to follow in reporting suspected cases.

Although the confidentiality of the counselor/client relationship may be violated, the school counselor has a duty to protect the minor child from harm. Most often, though, the child who is a victim of such abuse, and who reports it to the counselor, is seeking help. The skillful counselor seeks the consent of the child to report the incident or incidents in an effort to maintain a trusting relationship with the child.

The following excerpt from the Michigan Child Protection Law as well as other sections of relevant law can be found at the Michigan Legislature's website:

www.legislature.mi.gov/(S(m0mimx450sugae455durwqnl))/mileg.aspx?page =GetMCLDocument&objectname=mcl-Act-238-of-1975&version=txt.

CHILD PROTECTION LAW (EXCERPT)
Act 238 of 1975

722.623 Individual required to report child abuse or neglect; written report; transmitting report to county department; copies to prosecuting attorney and probate court; conditions requiring transmission of report to law enforcement agency; exposure to or contact with methamphetamine production; pregnancy of or venereal disease in child less than 12 years of age.

Sec. 3.

(1) An individual is required to report under this act as follows:

(a) A physician, dentist, physician's assistant, registered dental hygienist, medical examiner, nurse, person licensed to provide emergency medical care, audiologist, psychologist, marriage and family therapist, licensed professional counselor, social worker, licensed master's social worker, licensed bachelor's social worker, registered social service technician, social service technician, a person employed in a professional capacity in any office of the friend of the court, school administrator, school counselor or teacher, law enforcement officer, member of the clergy, or regulated child care provider who has reasonable cause to suspect child abuse or neglect shall make immediately, by telephone or otherwise, an oral report, or cause an oral report to be made, of the suspected child abuse or neglect to the department. Within 72 hours after making the oral report, the reporting person shall file a written report as required in this act. If the reporting person is a member of the staff of a hospital, agency, or school, the reporting person shall notify the person in charge of the hospital, agency, or school of his or her finding and that the report has been made, and shall make a copy of the written report available to the person in charge. A notification to the person in charge of a hospital, agency, or school does not relieve the member of the staff of the hospital, agency, or school of the obligation of reporting to the department as required by this section. One report from a hospital, agency, or school is adequate to meet the reporting requirement. A member of the staff of a hospital, agency, or school shall not be dismissed or otherwise penalized for making a report required by this act or for cooperating in an investigation.

(b) A department employee who is 1 of the following and has reasonable cause to suspect child abuse or neglect shall make a report of suspected child abuse or neglect to the department in the same manner as required under subdivision (a):

(i) Eligibility specialist.

(ii) Family independence manager.

(iii) Family independence specialist.

(iv) Social services specialist.

(v) Social work specialist.

(vi) Social work specialist manager.

(vii) Welfare services specialist.

(c) Any employee of an organization or entity that, as a result of federal funding statutes, regulations, or contracts, would be prohibited from reporting in the absence of a state mandate or court order. A person required to report under this subdivision shall report in the same manner as required under subdivision (a).

(2) The written report shall contain the name of the child and a description of the abuse or neglect. If possible, the report shall contain the names and addresses of the child's parents, the child's guardian, the persons with whom the child resides, and the child's age. The report shall contain other information available to the reporting person that might establish the cause of the abuse or neglect, and the manner in which the abuse or neglect occurred.

(3) The department shall inform the reporting person of the required contents of the written report at the time the oral report is made by the reporting person.

(4) The written report required in this section shall be mailed or otherwise transmitted to the county department of the county in which the child suspected of being abused or neglected is found.

(5) Upon receipt of a written report of suspected child abuse or neglect, the department may provide copies to the prosecuting attorney and the probate court of the counties in which the child suspected of being abused or neglected resides and is found.

(6) If an allegation, written report, or subsequent investigation of suspected child abuse or child neglect indicates a violation of sections 136b and 145c, sections 520b to 520g of the Michigan penal code, 1931 PA 328, MCL 750.136b, 750.145c, and 750.520b to 750.520g, or section 7401c of the public health code, 1978 PA 368, MCL

333.7401c, involving methamphetamine has occurred, or if the allegation, written report, or subsequent investigation indicates that the suspected child abuse or child neglect was committed by an individual who is not a person responsible for the child's health or welfare, including, but not limited to, a member of the clergy, a teacher, or a teacher's aide, the department shall transmit a copy of the allegation or written report and the results of any investigation to a law enforcement agency in the county in which the incident occurred. If an allegation, written report, or subsequent investigation indicates that the individual who committed the suspected abuse or neglect is a child care provider and the department believes that the report has basis in fact, the department shall, within 24 hours of completion, transmit a copy of the written report or the results of the investigation to the child care regulatory agency with authority over the child care provider's child care organization or adult foster care location authorized to care for a child.

(7) If a local law enforcement agency receives an allegation or written report of suspected child abuse or child neglect or discovers evidence of or receives a report of an individual allowing a child to be exposed to or to have contact with methamphetamine production, and the allegation, written report, or subsequent investigation indicates that the child abuse or child neglect or allowing a child to be exposed to or to have contact with methamphetamine production, was committed by a person responsible for the child's health or welfare, the local law enforcement agency shall refer the allegation or provide a copy of the written report and the results of any investigation to the county department of the county in which the abused or neglected child is found, as required by subsection (1)(a). If an allegation, written report, or subsequent investigation indicates that the individual who committed the suspected abuse or neglect or allowed a child to be exposed to or to have contact with methamphetamine production, is a child care provider and the local law enforcement agency believes that the report has basis in fact, the local law enforcement agency shall transmit a copy of the written report or the results of the investigation to the child care regulatory agency with authority over the child care provider's child care organization or adult foster care location authorized to care for a child. Nothing in this subsection or subsection (1) shall be construed to relieve the department of its responsibilities to investigate reports of suspected child abuse or child neglect under this act.

(8) For purposes of this act, the pregnancy of a child less than 12 years of age or the presence of a venereal disease in a child who is over 1 month of age but less than 12 years of age is reasonable cause to suspect child abuse and neglect have occurred.

(9) In conducting an investigation of child abuse or child neglect, if the department suspects that a child has been exposed to or has had contact with methamphetamine production, the department shall immediately contact the law enforcement agency in the county in which the incident occurred.

BIBLIOGRAPHY

BEST, J.W. & KAHN, J.V., (1996), *Research in Education,* 7th Edition. Boston: Allyn & Bacon, Inc.

BRAGSTAD, B.J., & STUMPF, S. M., (1987), *A Guidebook for Teaching Study Skills and Motivation,* 2nd Edition, Boston: Allyn & Bacon, Inc.

BROWNELL, J., (1986), *Building Active Listening Skills,* Englewood Cliffs, NJ: Prentice-Hall Inc.

BUKSTEIN, O.G., (1995), *Substance Abuse - Adolescent Assessment & Prevention,* John Wiley & Sons.

BURLEY-ALLEN, M., (1982), *Listening: The Forgotten Skill,* Hoboken, NJ: John Wiley & Sons, Inc.

CARTWRIGNT, D., & ZANDER, A., Editors, (1968), *Group Dynamics, Research & Theory,* 3rd Edition, New York: Harper & Row.

CATES, W.M., (1985), *A Practical Guide to Educational Research,* Englewood Cliffs, NJ: Prentice-Hall Inc.

COREY, G., (1991), *Manual For Theory & Practice of Counseling & Psychotherapy,* 4th Edition, Pacific Grove, CA: Brooks/Cole Publishing Co.

COREY, G., (1996), *Instructor's Manual for Theory & Practice of Counseling & Psychotherapy,* 5th Edition, Pacific Grove, CA: Brooks/Cole Publishing Co.

COREY, G., (1996), *Student Manual for Theory & Practice of Counseling & Psychotherapy,* 5th Edition, Pacific Grove, CA:, Brooks/Cole Publishing Co.

COREY, G., (1990), *Theory & Practice of Group Counseling,* 3rd Edition, Pacific Grove, CA: Brooks/Cole Publishing Co.

COTTLE, W.C., (1968), *Guidance Monograph Series, Series 111, Testing, Interest & Personality Inventories,* Boston: Houghton Mifflin Co.

DOUGHERTY, A.M., (1995), *Case Studies in Human Services Consultation,* Pacific Grove, CA: Brooks/Cole Publishing Co.

DOWNING, L.N., (1968), *Guidance & Counseling Services, An Introduction,* New York, McGraw-Hill Book Co.

DRESHMAN, J.L., CRABBE, C.L. & TARASEVICH, S. (2001), *Caring in Times of Crisis: A Crisis Management/Postvention Manual for Administrators, Student Assistance Teams & Other School Personnel K-12.* Chapin, SC: Youthlight, Inc.

DUNN, R. & DUNN, K., (1978), *Teaching Students through Their Individual Learning Styles, A Practical Approach,* Reston, VA: Reston Publishing Co.

ERIKSON, E.H., (1963), *Childhood & Society,* 2nd Edition, New York, W.W. Norton & Co. Inc.

GOLDMAN, L., (1961), *Century Psychology Series, Using Tests in Counseling,* New York, Appleton-Century Crofts.

GRESSARD, C.F., & KEEL, L. *Counseling Today,* February 1998, *Ethics in Counseling,* pg. 16.

GUERNSEY, T.F. & KLARE, K., (1993), *Special Education Law,* Durham, NC: Carolina Academic Press.

HAZLER, R.J., PH.D., (1996), *Breaking the Cycle of Violence,* Washington, DC: Accelerated Development.

HERGENHAHN B.R., (1988), *An Introduction to Theories of Learning,* 3rd Edition, Englewood Cliffs, NJ: Prentice-Hall Inc.

JOHNSON, D.W., JOHNSON, R.T., (1995), *Reducing School Violence through Conflict Resolution,* Alexandria, VA: Association for Supervision & Curriculum Development.

JOHNSON, D.W., & JOHNSON, F.P., (1975), *Joining Together, Group Theory & Group Skills,* Englewood Cliffs, NJ: Prentice-Hall Inc.

KEMP, C.G., (1964), *Perspectives on the Group Process,* Boston, Houghton Mifflin Co.

LYMAN, H.B., (1968), *Guidance Monograph Series, Series 111 Testing, Intelligence, Aptitude & Achievement Testing,* Boston: Houghton Mifflin Co.

MAHLER, C., CALDWELL, E., (1961), *Group Counseling in Secondary Schools,* Chicago, IL: Science Research Associates.

MAHLER, C., (1969). *Group Counseling in the School.* Boston: Houghton Mifflin Co.

MEYERING R.A., (1968), *Guidance Monograph Series,, Series 11 Counseling, Use of Test Data in Counseling,* Boston: Houghton Mifflin Co.

MCDANIELS, C., NORMAN, C.G., (1992), *Counseling for Career Development,* 1st Edition, San Francisco: Jossey-Bass Publishers.

Forum Guide to the Privacy of Student Information: A Resource for Schools (NFES 2006–805). (2006). U.S. Dept of Education. Washington, DC: National Center for Education Statistics.

OSIPOW, S.H., (1968), *Theories of Career Development,* New York, Century Psychology Series, Appleton-Century Crofts, Educational Division of Meredith Corp.

OSIPOW, S.H., FITZGERALD, L.F., (1996), *Theories of Career Development,* 4th Edition, Boston: Allyn & Bacon.

OSIPOW, S.H., & WALSH, W.B., (1970), *Strategies in Counseling for Behavior Change,* New York: Century Psychology Series, Appleton-Century Crofts.

PATTERSON, C.H., (1966), *Theories of Counseling & Psychotherapy,* New York, Harper-Row.

REEVES, E.T., (1970), *The Dynamics of Group Behavior,* New York: American Management Association, Inc.

ROGERS, D., (1969), *Readings in Child Psychology,* Pacific Groves, CA: Brooks/Cole Publishing Co.

SHAW, M.E., (1976), *Group Dynamics - The Psychology of Small Group Behavior,* 2nd Edition, New York: McGraw-Hill Book Co.

SIMS, R.R., & SIMS, S.J., (1995), *The Importance of Learning Styles,* Westport, CT: Greenwood Press.

VANDRACEK, R.M., LERNER, M.R., & SCHULENBERG, J.E., (1986), *Career Development: A Life Span Developmental Approach,* Hillsdale, NJ: Lawrence Erlbaum Associates.

WHITE, J., MULLIS, F., EARLEG, B., & BRIGMAN, G., (1995), *Consultation in Schools, The Counselors Role,* Portland, ME: J. Weston Walch.

YALOM, I.D. & LESZCZ, M. (2005). *The Theory and Practice of Group Psychotherapy, 5th edition.* NY: Basic Books.

ZEBROWITZ, L.A., (1990), *Social Perception,* Pacific Grove, CA: Brooks/Cole Publishers.

ZUNKER, V.G., (1994), *Using Assessment Results for Career Development,* 4th Edition. Pacific Grove, CA: Brooks/Cole Publishers.

Sample Test

Directions: Read each item and select the best response.

1. Erik Erikson would assert that a junior high student who frequently visits social networking Internet sites is experiencing which of the following stages of development: *(Average Rigor) (Competency 1.0)*

   A. Generativity vs. Stagnation

   B. Basic Trust vs. Basic Mistrust

   C. Identity vs. Role Confusion

   D. Ego Integrity vs. Despair

2. Jean, a high school counselor, has noticed that a number of her tenth grade students are failing their physical education classes, a course required for graduation. When she questions several students about their grades, she learns that they have been skipping class because "Coach doesn't even take roll." This trend can best be explained by examining the principles of which of the following: *(Rigorous) (Competency 1.0)*

   A. Developmental stages

   B. Behavior theory

   C. Ego identity

   D. Existentialism

3. An elementary school counselor working with a fifth grade class notices a number of physical and emotional changes in her students. Which of the following is *not* a common change among students around ages 9 or 10 years old:
   (Easy) (Competency 1.0)

   A. Hormonal shifts

   B. Growth spurts

   C. Additional teeth and a change in jaw size

   D. New body hair

4. Maggie, a second grade student, has begun to demonstrate new behaviors since the beginning of the school year. Which of the following indicates age-appropriate social development: *(Average Rigor)(Competency 1.0)*

   A. Engaging in a group game during recess

   B. Bringing her imaginary friend to school to play with her peers

   C. Crying each morning when she is dropped off at the bus stop

   D. Checking an email account using the classroom computer

5. A school counselor notices that one of her students has begun to slow in progress over the past few weeks in the areas of social and academic development. When assessing progress in light of child development concepts, developmental stages:
   (Average Rigor) (Competency 2.0)

   A. Clearly identify where a child falls in a specific area of growth

   B. Cannot be relied upon

   C. Are significantly different for boys and girls

   D. Serve as guideposts

6. When reflecting on factors that impact development, a school counselor should consider all of the following except:
   (Average Rigor) (Competency 2.0)

   A. Gender and race

   B. Religion

   C. Their caregivers' emotional availability

   D. Nutrition

7. A seventh grader mentions to her counselor that she is dealing with some extremely stressful issues and feels that these issues have begun to affect her school performance. All of the following stressors may be affecting her school performance except:
(Rigorous) (Competency 2.0)

   A. Mental health issues

   B. Having a single parent

   C. Losing a parent to death or divorce

   D. Being harassed at school

8. A high school counselor recently enrolled a homeless student. He has a number of concerns for the student and the family. The counselor is mainly concerned that homelessness may make it difficult for his new student to:
(Rigorous) (Competency 3.0)

   A. Get a job after high school

   B. Make friends at school

   C. Succeed in school

   D. Get to school and/or attend class

9. A school counselor is working with the parents of a child who suffers from a chronic medical condition who is able to attend school. Her concerns include all of the following except:
(Average Rigor) (Competency 3.0)

   A. The student is unlikely to succeed in a mainstreamed school environment.

   B. The student needs some special accommodations for physical activity.

   C. The school nurse should be involved in planning for the child's needs.

   D. The student may not be able to complete all the assignments within the usual time frame allotted.

10. When assessing how students learn, which of the following would not be considered as a significant factor:
(Easy) (Competency 4.0)

    A. Past experiences

    B. Environmental factors

    C. Psychosexual stages

    D. Mental processes

11. An elementary school counselor assessing the factors that may be contributing to a student's success should consider all of the following factors except:
    (Rigorous) (Competency 4.0)

    A. Class size

    B. Home attitude towards education

    C. Initial positive introduction to the school experience

    D. Addressing the specific of each child

12. Individual learning styles can be expressed in relation to all of the following except:
    (Average Rigor) (Competency 4.0)

    A. Environmental factors

    B. Emotional factors

    C. Intelligence quotients

    D. Sociological elements

13. A school counselor notices that one of her students seems to do poorly in classes where the teachers use lecture as a primary instructional method, but does well in classes that involve hands-on exploration of material. To understand this better, the counselor might explore the learning theories of which of the following theorists:
    (Rigorous) (Competency 4.0)

    A. Jean Piaget

    B. Noam Chomsky

    C. B. F. Skinner

    D. Howard Gardner

14. A middle school counselor planning a classroom guidance unit on study skills should include all of the following suggestions except:
    (Easy) (Competency 5.0)

    A. Learning the material and then putting it aside until there is an exam scheduled

    B. Studying every day at a certain time

    C. Taking good notes

    D. Reviewing frequently

15. Cognitive development can be encouraged by all of the following except:
(Average Rigor)
(Competency 5.0)

   A. Discussion of current events

   B. Rote memorization

   C. Using recently learned material in practical ways

   D. Linking new information to the student's current knowledge base

16. School counselors must assist students in making decisions while fostering autonomy. When helping students to make decisions, steps in the process do not include:
(Average Rigor)
(Competency 6.0)

   A. Defining the problem

   B. Listing all the options

   C. Surveying family, friends, and peers

   D. Formulating goals in relation to outcomes

Use this scenario to answer the next three questions (17-19):

Counselor: I understand that you and Sarah had an argument in Mrs. Tucker's room during class today. Can you tell me what happened?

Student: Sarah has been my best friend all this year in 7th grade. She told James that I like him after she promised she wouldn't tell him. Now he knows and everyone is laughing at me.

Counselor: So, what I'm hearing you say is that you shared your secret with Sarah thinking that you could trust her, and she shared your secret with other people. Is this how the argument started?

Student: No, we started fighting because she whispered something to James and they started laughing at me. So I told her to shut-up and then she yelled at me and that's what happened.

Counselor: And in the meantime, you disrupted Mrs. Tucker's teaching.

Student: I didn't really think about that...

Counselor: How do you think you could handle this situation in the future so that you don't end up in a fight with your friend, and you don't disrupt class?

17. The student's response to the counselor's initial statement indicates which of the following?
    (Rigorous) (Competency 6.0)

    A. The student recognizes her responsibility in the problem

    B. The student does not recognize her responsibility in the problem

    C. The student sees the problem as an issue between herself and her best friend

    D. She is too traumatized to return to the class with Sarah and James

18. The counselor's behavior throughout the session indicates that his objective was to facilitate:
    (Rigorous) (Competency 6.0)

    A. Conflict resolution between the student and Sarah

    B. A better understanding of the student's responsibility in the problem

    C. Modeling appropriate classroom behavior.

    D. A healthier understanding of the counseling process.

19. Based on the overall tone of the session, which of the following is the student MOST likely to do in the future?
    (Rigorous) (Competency 6.0)

    A. Return to class and resume the argument with Sarah

    B. Avoid returning to the counselor's office to resolve a problem

    C. Apologize to Mrs. Tucker for disrupting class

    D. Think about this experience before sharing additional personal information with Sarah

TEACHER CERTIFICATION STUDY GUIDE

20. School counselors must work with students to build trusting relationships. Effective communication is a key component in building relationships with students. The keys to effective communication include all of the following except:
(Average Rigor) (Competency 6.0)

   A. Being able to anticipate what the speaker is going to say

   B. Paying attention to nonverbal communication

   C. Asking for clarification

   D. Expressing oneself clearly and directly

21. Positive school environments have all of the following characteristics except:
(Easy) (Competency 6.0)

   A. Strict rules

   B. Clear adult leadership

   C. Respect for diversity

   D. Policies and procedures to ensure the safety of everyone in the school community

22. Which of the following is not a form of assessment administered by school counselors:
(Easy) (Competency 7.0)

   A. Achievement tests

   B. Intelligence tests

   C. College entrance exams

   D. Performance tests

23. A condition that does not affect testing results is:
(Average Rigor) (Competency 7.0)

   A. The physical and mental condition of the testee

   B. The testing room environment

   C. The colors of the clothes the proctors are wearing

   D. The validity of the test

GUIDANCE COUNSELOR 151

24. **Which of the following is NOT considered an advantage of testing:**
    (Average Rigor) (Competency 7.0)

    A. As a way to obtain multiple test interpretations

    B. As a way to help students recognize and use the resources they have

    C. As a way to present meaningful information to the student for decision making

    D. As a way to help identify options for the future

25. **Disadvantages of testing include all the following except:**
    (Rigorous) (Competency 7.0)

    A. The possibility of results being used improperly

    B. The possibility of the student misinterpreting the test results

    C. The inherent subjectivity of tests administered for counseling purposes

    D. Using the test to predict future behavior

26. **Informal forms of assessment include all of the following except:**
    (Average Rigor) (Competency 7.0)

    A. Behavioral observation

    B. Learning styles inventories

    C. Interviewing peers

    D. Sentence completion

27. **The inaccuracy of test results caused by chance is referred to as:**
    (Average Rigor) (Competency 7.0)

    A. Standardization

    B. Standard Error of Measurement

    C. Standard Score

    D. Derived Score

28. **A statistical concept that measures the relationship between two factors with regard to test validity is:**
    (Average Rigor) (Competency 7.0)

    A. Reliability Coefficient

    B. Standard Deviation

    C. Raw Score

    D. Correlation Coefficient

29. A high school counselor is the end-of-course examinations coordinator for her school. While preparing for test administration, she must follow all of the following procedures except: *(Easy) (Competency 8.0)*

   A. Safeguarding the tests

   B. Informing the students of the nature of the test by giving them questions from the test

   C. Guarding the tests in the exam room when students have access to the room

   D. Guarding the tests by not leaving them where students and non-authorized personnel have access

30. The written report of test results and interpretation should not: *(Average Rigor) (Competency 8.0)*

   A. Be written in understandable language

   B. Always include charts and graphs

   C. Be disseminated on a need to know basis

   D. Be written in the language of testing

31. A high school counselor is responsible for designing a workshop to help parents interpret test data. In order to ensure accurate test interpretation by others, he must follow all the following guidelines except: *(Rigorous) (Competency 8.0)*

   A. A uniform method of recording should be employed

   B. Consistency in language used should be employed

   C. The purpose, limitations, and the validity of the test should be stated

   D. The receiver of the results should be required to contact the counselor in order to receive the counselor's candid opinion

32. Joe's parents are concerned about Joe's performance in school and on recent achievement tests. He has been evaluated by an outside agency's psychologist regarding IQ and learning ability who believes he is underperforming. Which of the following would be the BEST next step for the school counselor?
(Rigorous) (Competency 9.0)

   A. Offer to meet with the student and his parents to review all the tests and explore what might be going on

   B. Offer to meet with the outside psychologist to review all the tests and explore what might be going on

   C. Ask the parents to have the outside psychologist send the test results to the school counselor

   D. Refer the parents back to the outside psychologist for further testing

33. If tests need to be interpreted in a group, the school counselor should not:
(Easy) (Competency 9.0)

   A. Announce individual test scores

   B. Explain the norm group to which the students have been compared

   C. Provide for private individual interpretation for students

   D. Explain statistics of the test so students can understand the meaning of their scores

34. **In helping a student plan her course of study, the counselor should review and interpret test results with the student. In doing so, the school counselor should not:** *(Average Rigor) (Competency 9.0)*

   A. Relate the results to the goals that had previously been determined

   B. Provide for individual interpretation

   C. Wait to interpret the tests when the student is scheduling the following year's courses

   D. Give the student input into the interpretation of the results

35. When interpreting test results for other professionals and parents, the school counselor is not required to:
    (Average Rigor)
    (Competency 9.0)

    A. Be thoroughly familiar with the test

    B. Let other staff members see the results of the test

    C. Notify the student that the counselor will be sharing the results with their parent/guardian(s)

    D. Work with the parents in a counseling relationship to help them understand their child's abilities

36. When interpreting testing data from other professionals and testing firms, the counselor should do all the following except:
    (Average Rigor) (Competency 9.0)

    A. Understand the material in the report

    B. Go right to the summary and not worry about the technical aspects of the report

    C. Contact the writer of the report for clarification if needed

    D. Refer to the testing manual for clarification if needed

Use this scenario to answer the next three questions (37-39):

Counselor: When we talked the other day, you shared with me that you overheard your parents discussing a divorce, and I know that was a very, very difficult thing for you to hear. How are you feeling today?

Student: I'm really angry at both of them, and I wish they would stop trying to pretend everything is okay.

Counselor: You mentioned that you felt more comfortable talking with your mom about the situation than your dad. Have you had an opportunity to talk with her about it?

Student: No, not yet. I just don't know what to say to her.

Counselor: Why don't we practice that today? Let's try this: Turn your chair to face this empty chair, and pretend that your mom is sitting right here in front of you. How do you feel about trying that?

Student: I don't know. It seems kind of weird, but I guess we could try.

37. **The student's response to the counselor's initial question indicates which of the following?**
    (Rigorous) (Competency 10.0)

    A. The student and counselor have established a comfortable rapport with one another

    B. The student does not have an accurate understanding of the situation between his parents

    C. The student is avoiding his own concerns by blaming the situation on his parents

    D. The student's anger at his parents hinders his ability to address school-related issues

38. The counselor's behavior throughout the session indicates that her objective was to: *(Rigorous) (Competency 10.0)*

    A. Encourage the student to take responsibility for his part in the problem

    B. Help the student learn to mediate the problems between his parents

    C. Help the student communicate his concerns more effectively

    D. Help the student work through his anger toward his parents

39. Suggesting the empty chair technique indicates that the counselor's objective was to do which of the following? *(Rigorous) (Competency 10.0)*

    A. To give the student a safe environment in which to express his concerns to his mother.

    B. To help the student practice working through his anger toward his mother before the actual confrontation.

    C. To show the student how irrational his behavior has become.

    D. To gain a better understanding of the situation between the student's parents.

40. Jason enters the school counselor's office distraught over a recent breakup with his girlfriend of 6 months. He tells the counselor that if he could just make better grades and if he could wear nicer clothes and have more friends, he could win back his girlfriend. The counselor begins by examining Jason's irrational thoughts, which is an example of which of the following theories:
    (Rigorous) (Competency 10.0)

    A. Reality Therapy

    B. Gestalt Therapy

    C. Rational Emotive Behavior Therapy

    D. Behavior Therapy

41. Alexandra is having difficulty relating to her classmates and often uses backstabbing as a mechanism to make friends. In a counseling session, the counselor confronts Alex with a number of details that push her to take responsibility for her own actions. This is an example of:
    (Rigorous) (Competency 10.0)

    A. Reality Therapy

    B. Existentialist Therapy

    C. Behavior Therapy

    D. Person-Centered Therapy

42. A school counselor is conducting small group sessions in which students participate in role-playing exercises to learn more effective communication skills. The small group offers all of the following except:
    (Average Rigor) (Competency 11.0)

    A. The presence of a built in support system

    B. A non-threatening atmosphere

    C. The substitution of the group for the real world, permitting clients unlimited time to make adjustments

    D. The counselor can reach more clients

43. A high school counselor is running an aggression replacement small group. Throughout the process, he has noted some positive outcomes of group counseling, as well as a few limitations. These limitations include all of the following except:
(Rigorous) (Competency 11.0)

   A. There is pressure to accept group values without analyzing them

   B. Some of the students are changing their behavior much more quickly than the others

   C. One of the students seems to have significant problems with impulse control in spite of the group's feedback

   D. A few individuals in the group are justifying their behavior due to reinforcement from the group

44. A middle school counselor is organizing a support group for students affected by a recent disaster – major flooding that displaced a number of families. Which of the following would be the least important in setting up this group?
(Rigorous) (Competency 11.0)

   A. Limiting the group to a specific grade level

   B. Limiting the group to no more than 10 students

   C. Seeking parental permission for student participation

   D. Ensuring that the students will be able to make up any school work from classes they miss when attending the group

45. A group of students in ninth grade have been fighting with each other. Upon meeting with the students, the counselor learns that many of the fights are precipitated by arguments between two groups of students who come from the two middle schools they previously attended. Which of the following group guidance approaches would be least appropriate in this situation?
(Rigorous) (Competency 12.0)

   A. Teaching core concepts about diversity and tolerance in a large group assembly

   B. Leading anger management sessions in a small group format

   C. Holding a meeting for parents and students to discuss the problem

   D. Training students in peer mediation

46. As part of the continued response to the situation in the previous question, the school counselor implements a violence prevention program. It utilizes all of the following interventions except:
(Average Rigor) (Competency 12.0)

   A. Conflict resolution seminars

   B. Behavior modification programs

   C. Training faculty and staff to intervene before violent confrontations occur

   D. Instituting a boxing program to train students to protect themselves

47. An elementary school counselor conducts a needs assessment to determine specific issues facing his students and the faculty of his school. In the process, he discovers that there is a need for a new program. The need for this specialized program may be indicated by each of the following factors except:
(Rigorous) (Competency 12.0)

    A. Increased classroom management problems

    B. Available grant money

    C. The completion of a formal needs assessment

    D. Teacher or counselor observations

48. A high school counselor plans to implement a peer-mentoring program. In order to ensure confidentiality, promote effectiveness, and foster a safe environment for all participants, she should:
(Average Rigor) (Competency 12.0)

    A. Not be present when students are conducting a group

    B. Choose the leaders from potential drop-outs

    C. Try not to let parents know what the process involves, so the students can have privacy

    D. Have the student leaders go through an extensive period of training by a professional

49. Data included in the initial referral of a child to a counselor should not include:
(Easy) (Competency 13.0)

    A. Unverified illegal behavior

    B. Academic history

    C. Behavior and discipline history

    D. Family history

50. Procedures for referring a student to an outside agency do not include this information:
(Easy) (Competency 13.0)

   A. The counselor believes there may be a need for long-term counseling

   B. The parent feels the child has an emotional problem and asks for an evaluation

   C. The counselor is mandated to report a sexual abuse case

   D. The student doesn't like the counselor

51. A school counselor creating a parent resource center in his office should make available which of the following resources for his clients:
(Easy) (Competency 13.0)

   A. Mental health referrals

   B. Food banks and government aid programs

   C. Local support groups

   D. All of the above

52. The death of a fourth grader in a sledding accident has prompted the implementation of the school crisis response plan. Which of the following would not be included as an appropriate activity in the plan: *(Easy) (Competency 14.0)*

   A. Getting accurate information out to all members of the school community

   B. Sharing the latest media reports about the accident with staff and students

   C. Offering crisis/grief counseling to all students

   D. Providing information to parents and guardians about common stress and grief reactions

53. A bomb threat is reported at the high school, and the school is evacuated. In order to function appropriately as a crisis responder in this situation, the school counselor needs all of the following except:
(Average Rigor)
(Competency 14.0)

A. A chance to debrief and get support from colleagues

B. Clarity about roles and responsibilities

C. Mandatory post-trauma counseling

D. Adequate training and follow-up

54. A school counselor is asked to develop a crisis management plan for her school. She includes all of the following in the plan except:
(Average Rigor)
(Competency 14.0)

A. Specific lines of communication

B. The name of the crisis team leader

C. Goals of the plan

D. Intervention strategies

55. A student enters the school counselor's office and displays signs of child abuse and neglect, which include all of the following except: *(Easy) (Competency 15.0)*

A. Old clothing

B. Frequent bone fractures

C. Self-destructive behavior

D. Poor hygiene

56. A seventh grade student reports to her counselor that she is concerned about a friend, whom she believes to be taking prescription medications that she purchases from a classmate. The counselor asks the student to elaborate on the reasons she believes her friend is using and deduces that she is correct based on all of the following indicators except: *(Easy) (Competency 15.0)*

A. Non-participation in athletic activities

B. Attention problems

C. Bizarre behavior

D. Unawareness of surroundings

57. A high school counselor is concerned that a female student has anorexia nervosa. She bases this hunch on all of the following except: *(Easy) (Competency 15.0)*

   A. Malnutrition

   B. Behavior regression

   C. No outward signs but observations of the student not eating lunch

   D. Recognizable weight loss

58. A counselor notices an eighth grade student who has begun to wear a jacket every day despite warm temperatures. She also knows the family has been stressed lately with several issues. When the counselor talks with the student, she discovers that the student is self-injuring. The student explains that she is cutting herself because she is: *(Average Rigor) (Competency 15.0)*

   A. Suicidal

   B. Overly focused on what others think of her

   C. Trying to get attention

   D. Expressing emotional pain in a physical way

59. In classroom discussion following a video on civil rights and violence, twelfth grade students express opinions about the effects of stereotyping and prejudice on victims. They determine these effects include all of the following except: *(Rigorous) (Competency 15.0)*

   A. The necessity to confront the perpetrator

   B. The development of a sense of inferiority

   C. The development of a persecution complex

   D. Thoughts of violence toward the perpetrator

60. Florita has recently enrolled in the high school after moving here from Guatemala. The school counselor has reached out to the parents but has not had much luck in getting a response to her overtures. In an effort to improve the situation, the counselor might do all of the following except:
(Rigorous)
(Competency 16.0)

   A. Get more information about Guatemalan culture and beliefs

   B. Talk with Florita about her parents' feelings about being in the U.S.

   C. Ask Florita about her parents' language needs

   D. Contact a counselor she knows who has worked with Latin American students for insight and information

61. A school counselor is confused by his repeated inability to connect with students of races other than his own. He feels that he is respectful and interested in them, but they and their parents/guardians, never seem to really talk with him or accept his suggestions. He attends a workshop on cultural competence and learns all of the following except:
(Rigorous) (Competency 16.0)

   A. The best way to become more culturally competent is to attend a series of workshops on the topic

   B. He needs to learn more about his students' cultural backgrounds

   C. He has made assumptions about what his students feel and think that are probably inaccurate

   D. Just being sensitive to differences isn't enough; it's only a first step

Use this scenario to answer the next three questions (62-64):

Counselor: You mentioned that you have some concerns about your coursework as far as the colleges to which you are applying. Walk me through your concerns, and we'll address them one at a time.

Student: Well, first of all, I was thinking that I only had to complete three Social Studies credits to graduate, but it looks like all of my college choices require four credits. What am I going to do to make up the fourth credit? I already have my schedule for next year, and I have seven classes already selected.

Counselor: Let's take a look at your schedule and see what we need to do. I see that you're planning to take Art and Choir next year, and from what I remember, you really enjoy fine arts courses.

Student: I really do want to take those fine arts classes. I think I may major in Art Education in college. I don't really want to drop either of those classes.

Counselor: I understand that you want to take both, so you're going to need to make a choice based on your goals and on what's best for you. You can take both art classes next year and possibly go to summer school for a Social Studies credit, or...

Student: No, I definitely don't want to go to summer school!

Counselor: Okay, we could look at colleges that only require three credits, or we could change one fine arts class to a Contemporary Issues or Psychology/Sociology course. If we do that, you would be able to meet your fourth requirement for Social Studies for your colleges. What do you think?

Student: Well, I really, really want to participate in both arts classes, but I think this is more important. I sing in my church choir, and I'm a member of Art Club. I guess I'll just take art and change my choir class to Contemporary Issues. I've heard that's a great class.

Counselor: That's an excellent choice. You'll really enjoy that class. What an easy fix! So, what's next?

62. The student's response to the counselor's initial suggestion for schedule changes indicates which of the following: *(Rigorous) (Competency 17.0)*

   A. The student is unwilling to consider the counselor's suggestions at this time

   B. The student is only interested in having fun

   C. The student is focusing more on minute details than on choices that directly affect his college plans

   D. The student sees the arts classes as more important to his future than the Social Studies classes

63. The counselor's objective throughout the session is which of the following: *(Rigorous) (Competency 17.0)*

   A. To influence the student to make choices based on his parents' wishes.

   B. To help the student to take responsibility for his decisions.

   C. To influence the student to make choices based on the counselor's wishes.

   D. To empower the student to make the best decision for himself based on several options.

64. Which of the following is MOST likely to occur following this session: *(Rigorous) (Competency 17.0)*

    A. Based on the success of his previous decision, the student will feel confident in making additional choices about his schedule.

    B. The student will feel as though the counselor is patronizing him.

    C. The student will make the rest of his decisions without input from the counselor.

    D. The student will feel obligated to ask for the counselor's help in making scheduling decisions in the future.

65. Similarities in theories of vocational choice are all of the following except: *(Average Rigor) (Competency 18.0)*

    A. They describe the relationship between two sets of observations

    B. They incorporate a variety of theories

    C. They consider family influence on vocational choice a primary consideration

    D. They are usually based upon personality theory

66. An eighth grade student reports to her counselor that she will be working with a political campaign to earn volunteer hours for her philanthropy club. Her responsibilities will include designing yard signs and going door to door to meet potential voters. It is likely that she would be categorized under which occupational environments based on Holland's theory: *(Rigorous) (Competency 18.0)*

   A. Artistic and social

   B. Realistic and investigative

   C. Enterprising and investigative

   D. Social and conventional

67. A school counselor finds Super's theory of vocations helpful in working with students on exploring career choices. This theory is based upon all of the following except: *(Average Rigor) (Competency 18.0)*

   A. The inheritance of psychic energies

   B. The development of self-concepts

   C. External conditions that dictate the expression of self-concepts vocationally

   D. Developmental behavior theory

68. While presenting a career exploration unit with eleventh grade students, a school counselor arranges for her students to participate in a job shadowing experience. When preparing the students, she says that the experience should include all of the following except: *(Easy) (Competency 19.0)*

   A. Spending an extended period of time with a particular person in a chosen field

   B. Being paid

   C. A learning experience by the student and the business volunteer

   D. Experiencing the daily routine of a particular business

69. The role of the counselor in assisting students in exploring career and educational options includes all the following except: *(Average Rigor) (Competency 19.0)*

   A. Have material for exploration easily accessible

   B. Support and encourage students in their search for career choices

   C. Help students form realistic decisions

   D. Explain career choice theories to them

70. The school counselor has determined that a number of eleventh graders are interested in learning how to write a resume. Which of the following is the least appropriate method for teaching these skills?
(Rigorous) (Competency 19.0)

   A. Working with the teachers in the English and business education departments on a unit on resume writing skills to be co-taught by the two departments

   B. Planning a large group assembly to teach the latest methods and styles of resumes utilizing a well-developed PowerPoint presentation

   C. Offering a three-session program on resume-writing for every study hall period over the next two months

   D. Offering a two-session program on resume-writing to be conducted in all eleventh grade English or social studies classes

71. The business education teacher has approached the school counselor to help him with teaching job-interviewing skills. Following a lecture and discussion of key skills, which of the following would be the most effective approach?
(Rigorous) (Competency 19.0)

   A. A role play by the counselor and teacher on how to do a good interview

   B. A role play by the counselor and teacher, followed by a discussion of the students' fears and concerns about interviewing for a job

   C. A role play by the counselor and teacher, followed by practice role plays by the student

   D. A role play by the counselor and teacher, followed by a computerized search of jobs in the students' area of interest

72. Decision making occurs at all the following critical points in career development except:
    (Average Rigor) (Competency 20.0)

    A. When a student enters high school

    B. In selecting an entry level job

    C. When selecting education plans

    D. In changing jobs

73. **A high school counselor is creating a career education center in her office, which will include written materials, games, interest inventories, and computers designated for career exploration. She is in the process of evaluating materials to be included in her career center. She looks for all of the following except:**
    (Average Rigor)
    (Competency 20.0)

    A. Appropriate vocabulary for the targeted age and reading level

    B. Verified accuracy of the information

    C. Advertisements for career exploration tools

    D. The avoidance of biased and stereotyping images

74. The career information should include all of the following areas except:
    (Average Rigor)
    (Competency 20.0)

    A. The impressions of the reader as indicated by filling out an evaluation form

    B. The preparation required for entry level jobs

    C. The work setting and conditions of the career

    D. The long-term employment outlook

75. An eighth grader is very interested in both science and music. She is thinking about her schedule for ninth grade and is uncertain which choices to consider regarding classes. She visits her school counselor to think this through. Which of the following options would be most appropriate?
(Rigorous) (Competency 20.0)

   A. The counselor suggests the student take the basic courses in ninth grade science to see how she does before committing herself to any plan of action.

   B. The counselor discusses a career interest inventory tool with the student, and offers to meet with the student once it has been completed and scored, so they can discuss the student's options based on more information.

   C. The counselor recommends intelligence testing by the school psychologist to determine the student's capacity for science and music.

   D. The counselor signs the student up for as two science classes and high school chorus for ninth grade, telling the student that this plan will put her on track for the most options in the future.

76. Post secondary education opportunities are not offered in:
   (Average Rigor) (Competency 21.0)

   A. Vocational training

   B. Community colleges

   C. The military

   D. Practical experience

77. Post-secondary educational opportunities do not depend on: *(Average Rigor) (Competency 21.0)*

   A. The type of career in which the individual has an interest

   B. The abilities of the individual

   C. The social status of the individual

   D. The costs involved in attending

78. **Reliable sources of information on scholarships and financial aid do not include:** *(Easy) (Competency 21.0)*

   A. The guidance counselor

   B. Local scholarships

   C. Newspaper advertisements and paid financial aid sources

   D. Local and guidance department libraries

79. **Financial aid specifically earmarked for women and minorities is least likely to be found in:** *(Average Rigor) (Competency 21.0)*

   A. General financial aid references

   B. Minority and women's organizations

   C. The publication "The Higher Education Money Book for Women and Minorities"

   D. Local minority houses of worship

80. **When conducting a needs assessment, a school counselor should request input from which of the following:** *(Rigorous) (Competency 22.0)*

   A. Students only

   B. Administrators only

   C. People in the community who have no students in school

   D. The community, students, staff, administrators, and parents

81. **A school counselor evaluating the effectiveness of specific programs should consider all of the following except:** *(Rigorous) (Competency 22.0)*

   A. How well the program fits preconceived ideas of intended outcomes

   B. Statistical significance

   C. Interpretation of the meaning of the results

   D. The practicality of implementing the program into every day use

82. **Program objectives are:**
    (Average Rigor)
    (Competency 22.0)

    A. Created to fit the outcomes of the research

    B. Readjusted as the need arises

    C. Determined after the program has been operational for a period of time

    D. Formulated before the research is instituted

83. **In his first year at a new elementary school, a school counselor is excited to implement a number of new programs with his students. In order to implement the most effective programs, the counselor should begin by doing which of the following:**
    (Rigorous) (Competency 22.0)

    A. Ask the administration for a budget for the program

    B. Conduct a needs assessment survey

    C. Arrange for a pilot program

    D. Contact Board of Education members to get them to agree on the implementation of the program

84. **Choose the best answer in evaluating the following statement:** *(Rigorous)* *(Competency 23.0)*

    Counselor: (to a teacher) "Do you mind if I ask you about Shandra? She came to me with something personal and I'm not sure what to do. Can we talk?"

    A. Appropriate, because the teacher knows Shandra and her family quite well and may provide some insight.

    B. Appropriate, because the counselor needs to get a second opinion.

    C. Inappropriate, because counselors need to respect students' privacy and not discuss personal matters with teachers. An appropriate consult would be with another counselor.

    D. Inappropriate, because the teacher knows the student personally.

85. Choose the best answer in evaluating the counselor's statements in the following scenario:
(Rigorous) (Competency 23.0)

Student: *"Is it okay to talk with you about something private? I mean, do you have to tell someone else anything I tell you? This is really important."*

Counselor: *"I'm glad you came to me. I keep private everything students tell me, unless you are in danger of hurting yourself or someone else. Then I have to tell someone – that's the law. But let's see what's going on. I really would like to help you."*

Student: *"But you might have to tell someone. Maybe I shouldn't talk to you."*

Counselor: *"I will do my best to keep this between us. And I will tell you first if I need to go to someone else, including your parents. In fact, if I call your parents, I would like you to be in the room with me. How's that? We will only go to someone else if we have to. I really want to help."*

A. Appropriate, because she tells the student that she really wants to help her no matter what.

B. Appropriate, because the counselor is both reassuring about the importance of privacy and also honest about the need to disclosure certain information to parents and others.

C. Inappropriate, because the counselor creates anxiety by mentioning the law and possible disclosure.

D. Inappropriate, because the student will feel betrayed by the possible need to disclose the information.

86. **In implementing the Michigan Comprehensive Guidance and Counseling Program, a school district does not need to:**
(Average Rigor)
(Competency 24.0)

   A. Write a specific mission statement consistent with the school district's mission statement and purpose

   B. Provide all four components of the program (guidance curriculum, individual planning, responsive services and systems support) to all grade levels as long as adequate and developmentally appropriate guidance services are provided at each grade level

   C. Do a needs assessment and conduct periodic evaluations of the program for ongoing improvement

   D. Do a needs assessment and have an action plan for implementation

87. **An elementary school counselor is involved with helping families new to the district become acquainted with local resources for their children. This work falls under which component of the Michigan Comprehensive Guidance and Counseling Program:**
(Average Rigor)
(Competency 24.0)

   A. Guidance Curriculum

   B. Individual Planning

   C. Responsive Services

   D. Systems Support

88. Which of the following activities fall outside the scope of the Guidance Curriculum as outlined in the Michigan Comprehensive Guidance and Counseling Program:
(Rigorous) (Competency 24.0)

   A. Career Day, psycho-educational group on emotional intelligence, and classes on study skills

   B. Study skills support group, peer counseling program, and on-site college visits

   C. Socio-cultural sensitivity training, computerized career information searches, and mock job interviews

   D. School-to-work programs, personal counseling, and assemblies on violence prevention

89. The counseling department of a school district conducts a one day professional development session for all of the counselors in the entire district. Following this initial meeting, the district determines that this event should be repeated on an annual basis, at minimum. Counselors report all of the following positive results except:
(Easy) (Competency 25.0)

   A. They are kept abreast of changes in professional practices and standards

   B. They are able to utilize all available monies in the budget for staff development

   C. They are able to be refreshed and renewed as professionals

   D. They are able to further develop counseling skills

Use this scenario as a backdrop to answer the next five questions (90-94):

A first-year school counselor realizes early in the school year that she must learn to work closely with the administration, faculty, staff and parents of her students in order to most effectively serve her young students. She begins by administering a needs assessment to all stakeholders and then shares the carefully researched results in a faculty meeting. She requests permission from teachers of various subjects and grade levels to observe classes. When a teacher requests her assistance in working with specific students, she involves that teacher in the process by asking for his or her observations before, during, and after the observation. She also asks for help from her colleagues at other schools for prevention and intervention ideas, as well as ways to promote the school counseling program for the benefit of everyone involved. Before long, she notices that her counselor log is full of appointments, her interventions are becoming more successful, and she can no longer walk down the hall without receiving multiple greetings and questions from teachers, students, and parents.

90. **Procedures in the consultation process include all except:**
    (Average Rigor)
    (Competency 25.0)

    A. Relationship building

    B. Monitoring of the process of behavior change by a neutral party

    C. Evaluation and summarization

    D. Diagnosis of the problem

91. **The role the counselor can take in assisting participants in the consultation process does not include:**
    (Rigorous) (Competency 25.0)

    A. Demonstrating classroom behavior management techniques

    B. Describing the nature of the problem

    C. Teaching specific skills

    D. Helping devise strategies to change behaviors

92. **In the consultation process, communicating student's needs to others does not include:**
(Average Rigor)
(Competency 25.0)

    A. Making a judgment by the counselor to others as to what is best for the student

    B. Clarifying the needs of the student with the student

    C. Opening lines of communication between the consultee and the student by having open dialogue

    D. Balancing the needs of the student and the consultee so each can understand the other's position

93. **In conducting a consultation follow-up, the counselor should not:**
(Rigorous) (Competency 25.0)

    A. Gradually decrease participation in the process

    B. Reevaluate after a period of time

    C. Interview the consultee to determine if there is continuing progress

    D. Interview the student and parents in regards to their satisfaction with the consultation

94. **In evaluating the results of consultation, all the following factors should be considered except:**
(Rigorous) (Competency 25.0)

    A. The feelings of the student's parents as to the success of the process

    B. The report of the consultee as to the problem solving results

    C. An attitude change in the student

    D. Empirical results of an evaluation tool

95. **A good orientation program should include each of the following except:**
(Easy) (Competency 26.0)

    A. Advance notice by mail

    B. A tour of the facilities

    C. Invitations to the entire community

    D. Introduction of counselors and administrators to students and parents with a description of their roles

96. When a tenth grade student receives several disciplinary referrals in a short time period, her counselor contacts her parents in order to explain the situation and brainstorm solutions. Throughout the process, the counselor should do all of the following except: *(Rigorous) (Competency 26.0)*

   A. Inform the parents frequently as to the progress of the resolution of the problem

   B. Use parents as a valuable source of information about the student

   C. Accept parents' ideas for behavior modification

   D. Explain the problem in simple language as parents are probably unaware of all ramifications

97. A middle school counselor collaborating with parents in the counseling process for their seventh grade student should expect that the parents will contribute which of the following: *(Easy) (Competency 26.0)*

   A. Solutions to the presenting problem

   B. Family and medical history, a willingness to participate and possible solutions

   C. Very little, since most parents are uncooperative

   D. Monitoring the child at home

98. In working with parents, a good model to utilize is: *(Easy) (Competency 26.0)*

   A. Collaborative consultation

   B. Mental health consultation

   C. Family counseling

   D. Advising

99. The rights of parents, students, and guardians do not include:
(Average Rigor) (Competency 27.0)

A. Right of access

B. Right of privacy

C. Right to challenge and a hearing

D. Right to alter the written record if they feel it is not true

100. Written permission must be obtained to release assessment data from:
(Average Rigor) (Competency 27.0)

A. The counselor

B. The student over 18 or the student's parent or guardian

C. The Board of Education

D. The teacher who generated the assessment data

Answer Key

1. C	26. C	51. D	76. D
2. B	27. B	52. B	77. C
3. C	28. D	53. C	78. C
4. A	29. B	54. B	79. A
5. D	30. B	55. A	80. D
6. B	31. D	56. A	81. A
7. B	32. A	57. C	82. D
8. D	33. A	58. D	83. B
9. A	34. C	59. A	84. C
10. C	35. B	60. B	85. B
11. A	36. B	61. A	86. B
12. C	37. A	62. C	87. C
13. D	38. C	63. D	88. D
14. A	39. A	64. A	89. B
15. B	40. C	65. C	90. B
16. C	41. A	66. A	91. A
17. C	42. C	67. A	92. A
18. B	43. B	68. B	93. A
19. D	44. A	69. D	94. D
20. A	45. C	70. B	95. C
21. A	46. D	71. C	96. D
22. B	47. B	72. A	97. B
23. C	48. D	73. C	98. A
24. A	49. A	74. A	99. D
25. D	50. D	75. B	100. B

Rigor Table

	Easy %20	Average Rigor %40	Rigorous %40
Question #	3, 10, 14, 21, 22, 29, 33, 49, 50, 51, 52, 55, 56, 57, 68, 78, 89, 95, 97, 98	1, 4, 5, 6, 9, 12, 15, 16, 20, 23, 24, 26, 27, 28, 30, 34, 35, 36, 42, 46, 48, 53, 54, 58, 65, 67, 69, 72, 73, 74, 76, 77, 79, 82, 86, 87, 90, 92, 99, 100	2, 7, 8, 11, 13, 17, 18, 19, 25, 31, 32, 37, 38, 39, 40, 41, 43, 44, 45, 47, 59, 60, 61, 62, 63, 64, 66, 70, 71, 75, 80, 81, 83, 84, 85, 88, 91, 93, 94, 96

TEACHER CERTIFICATION STUDY GUIDE

Sample Test Answers and Rationales

Directions: Read each item and select the best response.

1. **Erik Erikson would assert that a junior high student who frequently visits social networking Internet sites is experiencing which of the following stages of development:**
   (Average Rigor) (Competency 1.0)

    A. Generativity vs. Stagnation

    B. Basic Trust vs. Basic Mistrust

    C. Identity vs. Role Confusion

    D. Ego Integrity vs. Despair

Answer: C. Identity vs. Role Confusion

According to Erik Erikson, Identity vs. Role Confusion occurs during adolescence and would be the only appropriate choice when referring to junior high students. The other options refer to very early childhood or adult developmental stages.

2. **Jean, a high school counselor, has noticed that a number of her tenth grade students are failing their physical education classes, a course required for graduation. When she questions several students about their grades, she learns that they have been skipping class because "Coach doesn't even take roll." This trend can best be explained by examining the principles of which of the following:**
   (Rigorous) (Competency 1.0)

    A. Developmental stages

    B. Behavior theory

    C. Ego identity

    D. Existentialism

Answer: B. Behavior theory
The students who are failing have been conditioned to believe that the coach only notices their absences when he takes attendance. For these students, the benefits of attending P.E. do not outweigh the risks of skipping class. They are responding to the conditioning they have experienced. These are basic principals of behavior theory.

TEACHER CERTIFICATION STUDY GUIDE

3. An elementary school counselor working with a fifth grade class notices a number of physical and emotional changes in her students. Which of the following is *not* a common change among students around ages 9 or 10 years old:
   (Easy) (Competency 1.0)

   A. Hormonal shifts

   B. Growth spurts

   C. Additional teeth and a change in jaw size

   D. New body hair

Answer: C. Additional teeth and a change in jaw size
At preadolescence (beginning around age 9 years and lasting till puberty), children experience hormonal shifts, growth spurts and new body hair. However, they do not experience a change in their jaw size.

4. Maggie, a second grade student, has begun to demonstrate new behaviors since the beginning of the school year. Which of the following indicates age-appropriate social development:
   (Average Rigor) (Competency 1.0)

   A. Engaging in a group game during recess

   B. Bringing her imaginary friend to school to play with her peers

   C. Crying each morning when she is dropped off at the bus stop

   D. Checking an email account using the classroom computer

Answer: A. Engaging in a group game during recess
Bringing an imaginary friend to school is a behavior that might be expected from a younger student. Crying each morning indicates separation anxiety, which is not developmentally appropriate for a student who has presumably been attending school regularly for two to three years. Checking an email account is a behavior that is appropriate for an older student. Therefore, answer A is the best answer.

GUIDANCE COUNSELOR

TEACHER CERTIFICATION STUDY GUIDE

5. A school counselor notices that one of her students has begun to slow in progress over the past few weeks in the areas of social and academic development. When assessing progress in light of child development concepts, developmental stages:
   (Average Rigor) (Competency 2.0)

   A. Clearly identify where a child falls in a specific area of growth

   B. Cannot be relied upon

   C. Are significantly different for boys and girls

   D. Serve as guideposts

Answer: D. Serve as guideposts
Developmental milestones are guideposts against which children's growth and developmental can be measured. They are not set in stone but do provide generally reliable markers. Although there are some gender differences, especially at preadolescence, overall boys and girls follow similar developmental pathways.

6. When reflecting on factors that impact development, a school counselor should consider all of the following except:
   (Average Rigor) (Competency 2.0)

   A. Gender and race

   B. Religion

   C. heir caregivers' emotional availability

   D. Nutrition

Answer: B. Religion
Development is affected by many different factors, one of which is generally NOT religion. Religion only affects development when specific religious practices or beliefs directly affect social and peer group interactions. Religion, per se, does not influence development.

7. A seventh grader mentions to her counselor that she is dealing with some extremely stressful issues and feels that these issues have begun to affect her school performance. All of the following stressors may be affecting her school performance except:
(Rigorous) (Competency 2.0)

    A. Mental health issues

    B. Having a single parent

    C. Losing a parent to death or divorce

    D. Being harassed at school

Answer: B. Having a single parent
Being the child of a single parent is not a stressor in and of itself. Losing a parent to death or divorce, coping with mental health or addiction issues at home, experiencing difficulties at school with peers, child abuse and others issues generally are stressors for children that affect school performance.

8. A high school counselor recently enrolled a homeless student. He has a number of concerns for the student and the family. The counselor is mainly concerned that homelessness may make it difficult for his new student to:
(Rigorous) (Competency 3.0)

    A. Get a job after high school

    B. Make friends at school

    C. Succeed in school

    D. Get to school and/or attend class

Answer: D. Get to school and/or attend class
Post-traumatic stress, poverty and other life concerns may interfere with a student's attendance. She or he may not come to school or may have difficulty paying attention in class. However, students from all families can succeed in school, make friends, and get a job after high school with the right support and motivation.

TEACHER CERTIFICATION STUDY GUIDE

9. A school counselor is working with the parents of a child who suffers from a chronic medical condition who is able to attend school. Her concerns include all of the following except:
   (Average Rigor) (Competency 3.0)

   A. The student is unlikely to succeed in a mainstreamed school environment

   B. The student needs some special accommodations for physical activity

   C. The school nurse should be involved in planning for the child's needs

   D. The student may not be able to complete all the assignments within the usual time frame allotted

Answer: A. The student is unlikely to succeed in a mainstreamed school environment.
Many students with special needs do best in a mainstream classroom, although they may need accommodations regarding physical activities, the time required to complete assignments or take tests, or other needs. Generally, the school nurse is part of the team working with students who have medical conditions.

10. When assessing how students learn, which of the following would not be considered as a significant factor:
    (Easy) (Competency 4.0)

    A. Past experiences

    B. Environmental factors

    C. Psychosexual stages

    D. Mental processes

Answer: C. Psychosexual stages
Psychosexual stages are a concept in psychoanalytic theory and are not included in discussions of learning theories.

11. An elementary school counselor assessing the factors that may be contributing to a student's success should consider all of the following factors except:
   (Rigorous) (Competency 4.0)

   A. Class size

   B. Home attitude towards education

   C. Initial positive introduction to the school experience

   D. Addressing the specific needs of each child

Answer: A. Class size
County or district guidelines may make stipulations on how many students may be in a classroom. However, the success of a student can involve many but class size is not one of these factors. This is a common educational misconception.

12. Individual learning styles can be expressed in relation to all of the following except:
   (Average Rigor) (Competency 4.0)

   A. Environmental factors

   B. Emotional factors

   C. Intelligence quotients

   D. Sociological elements

Answer: C. Intelligence quotients
Individual learning styles include environmental, emotional, sociological and physical elements. Learning styles do not measure and are not based on intelligence.

TEACHER CERTIFICATION STUDY GUIDE

13. **A school counselor notices that one of her students seems to do poorly in classes where the teachers use lecture as a primary instructional method, but does well in classes that involve hands-on exploration of material. To understand this better, the counselor might explore the learning theories of which of the following theorists:**
    (Rigorous) (Competency 4.0)

    A. Jean Piaget

    B. Noam Chomsky

    C. B. F. Skinner

    D. Howard Gardner

Answer: D. Howard Gardner
Gardner's theory of multiple intelligences describes individual learning styles based on different kinds of intelligence or aptitude. Some students are more inclined to learn through auditory methods, while others do better with kinesthetic approaches.

14. **A middle school counselor planning a classroom guidance unit on study skills should include all of the following suggestions except:**
    (Easy) (Competency 5.0)

    A. Learning the material and then putting it aside until there is an exam scheduled

    B. Studying every day at a certain time

    C. Taking good notes

    D. Reviewing frequently

Answer: A. Learning the material and then putting it aside until there is an exam scheduled
The student will not retain the information if there is a large gap between the learning and the testing of the material. The other suggestions have been shown to be effective study skills.

15. **Cognitive development can be encouraged by all of the following except:**
    (Average Rigor) (Competency 5.0)

    A. Discussion of current events

    B. Rote memorization

    C. Using recently learned material in practical ways

    D. Linking new information to the student's current knowledge base

Answer: B. Rote memorization
While there is a place for rote memorization in learning, it does not facilitate actual cognitive development as do the activities in options A, C, and D.

16. **School counselors must assist students in making decisions while fostering autonomy. When helping students to make decisions, steps in the process do not include:**
    (Average Rigor) (Competency 6.0)

    A. Defining the problem

    B. Listing all the options

    C. Surveying family, friends, and peers

    D. Formulating goals in relation to outcomes

Answer: C. Surveying family, friends, and peers
Surveying denotes a process of information gathering from friends and family; it is not a step in the decision making process.

TEACHER CERTIFICATION STUDY GUIDE

Use this scenario to answer the next three questions (17-19):

Counselor: I understand that you and Sarah had an argument in Mrs. Tucker's room during class today. Can you tell me what happened?

Student: Sarah has been my best friend all this year in 7th grade. She told James that I like him after she promised she wouldn't tell him. Now he knows and everyone is laughing at me.

Counselor: So, what I'm hearing you say is that you shared your secret with Sarah thinking that you could trust her, and she shared your secret with other people. Is this how the argument started?

Student: No, we started fighting because she whispered something to James and they started laughing at me. So I told her to shut-up and then she yelled at me and that's what happened.

Counselor: And in the meantime, you disrupted Mrs. Tucker's teaching.

Student: I didn't really think about that...

Counselor: How do you think you could handle this situation in the future so that you don't end up in a fight with your friend, and you don't disrupt class?

17. The student's response to the counselor's initial statement indicates which of the following?
    (Rigorous) (Competency 6.0)

    A. The student recognizes her responsibility in the problem

    B. The student does not recognize her responsibility in the problem

    C. The student sees the problem as an issue between herself and her best friend

    D. She is too traumatized to return to the class with Sarah and James

Answer: C. The student sees the problem as an issue between herself and her best friend
At this point, the only thing being discussed is the issue that brought the student to the counselor's office. There has been no mention of responsibility for the problem. The student does not feel as though she is being blamed, so A would not be an appropriate choice.

18. The counselor's behavior throughout the session indicates that his objective was to facilitate:
    (Rigorous) (Competency 6.0)

    A. Conflict resolution between the student and Sarah

    B. A better understanding of the student's responsibility in the problem

    C. Modeling appropriate classroom behavior.

    D. A healthier understanding of the counseling process.

Answer: B. A better understanding of the student's responsibility in the problem
The counselor's objective was to point out to the student that her behavior disrupted Mrs. Tucker's class. Options C and D are possible residual effects of the session. There was no mention of conflict resolution during the session, which would require the presence of both the student and her friend, Sarah.

19. Based on the overall tone of the session, which of the following is the student MOST likely to do in the future?
    (Rigorous) (Competency 6.0)

    A. Return to class and resume the argument with Sarah

    B. Avoid returning to the counselor's office to resolve a problem

    C. Apologize to Mrs. Tucker for disrupting class

    D. Think about this experience before sharing additional personal information with Sarah

Answer: D. Think about this experience before sharing additional personal information with Sarah
Developmentally, a 7th grade student is not typically mature enough to apologize to the teacher for disrupting a class. Additionally, the tone of the session does not indicate that the student wishes to continue the argument with Sarah or to retaliate against her. The session seems comfortable for the student, so it is unlikely that she will avoid additional visits to the counselor's office.

TEACHER CERTIFICATION STUDY GUIDE

20. School counselors must work with students to build trusting relationships. Effective communication is a key component in building relationships with students. The keys to effective communication include all of the following except:
    (Average Rigor) (Competency 6.0)

    A. Being able to anticipate what the speaker is going to say

    B. Paying attention to nonverbal communication

    C. Asking for clarification

    D. Expressing oneself clearly and directly

Answer: A. Being able to anticipate what the speaker is going to say
Focusing of what you *think* the speaker is going to say interferes with your ability to actually listen to what the speaker is saying.

21. Positive school environments have all of the following characteristics except:
    (Easy) (Competency 6.0)

    A. Strict rules

    B. Clear adult leadership

    C. Respect for diversity

    D. Policies and procedures to ensure the safety of everyone in the school community

Answer: A. Strict rules
While clear policies and strong leadership are essential, strict rules generally do not contribute to creating positive school environments. At times, they may even have a detrimental effect, depending on the nature of the rules.

22. **Which of the following is not a form of assessment administered by school counselors:**
    (Easy) (Competency 7.0)

    A. Achievement tests

    B. Intelligence tests

    C. College entrance exams

    D. Performance tests

Answer: B. Intelligence tests

Intelligence tests are generally administered by school psychologists, or psychologists in agencies or the private sector who are trained to do psychological testing.

23. **A condition that does not affect testing results is:**
    (Average Rigor) (Competency 7.0)

    A. The physical and mental condition of the testee

    B. The testing room environment

    C. The colors of the clothes the proctors are wearing

    D. The validity of the test

Answer: C. The colors of the clothes the proctors are wearing
There is no empirical research to date concerning the impact of the colors of the clothes the proctor is wearing on testing results. In addition to the physical and mental condition of the testee, the testing room environment and the preparation of the testee are conditions that can impact testing results as defined by research.

TEACHER CERTIFICATION STUDY GUIDE

24. Which of the following is NOT considered an advantage of testing: *(Average Rigor) (Competency 7.0)*

    A. As a way to obtain multiple test interpretations

    B. As a way to help students recognize and use the resources they have

    C. As a way to present meaningful information to the student for decision making

    D. As a way to help identify options for the future

Answer: A. As a away to get multiple test interpretations
One of the benefits of testing is to use a standardized process to provide information about the student's performance, access to success and to make recommendations.

25. Disadvantages of testing include all the following except: *(Rigorous) (Competency 7.0)*

    A. The possibility of results being used improperly

    B. The possibility of the student misinterpreting the test results

    C. The inherent subjectivity of tests administered for counseling purposes

    D. Using the test to predict future behavior

Answer: D. Using the test to predict future behavior
One of the purposes of testing is to provide a picture of where the student is currently and to anticipate what the student needs to in order to succeed in the future. The process may include identifying barriers to learning, tools needed to increase access to learning and potentially highlighting a process that would be beneficial to the student. However, tests cannot predict future behavior with any certainty.

26. Informal forms of assessment include all of the following except: *(Average Rigor) (Competency 7.0)*

    A. Behavioral observation

    B. Learning styles inventories

    C. Interviewing peers

    D. Sentence completion

Answer: C. Interviewing peers

Talking with a student's peers may provide information in a casual context that the school counselor may find useful, but this is not a form of assessment, either formal or informal.

27. The inaccuracy of test results caused by chance is referred to as: *(Average Rigor) (Competency 7.0)*

    A. Standardization

    B. Standard Error of Measurement

    C. Standard Score

    D. Derived Score

Answer: B. Standard Error of Measurement

Every test has some element of inaccuracy or unreliability due to chance so this element of the test is taken into consideration when evaluating test results and an allowance is made for this phenomenon. The degree of error is reported in the standard deviation, a specific band of scores. The formula for obtaining the standard error of measurement takes the square root of 1 minus the reliability coefficient.

TEACHER CERTIFICATION STUDY GUIDE

28. **A statistical concept that measures the relationship between two factors with regard to test validity is:**
    (Average Rigor) (Competency 7.0)

    A. Reliability Coefficient

    B. Standard Deviation

    C. Raw Score

    D. Correlation Coefficient

Answer: D. Correlation Coefficient
The reliability coefficient is a statistical concept that measures how reliable the relationship is between two factors in test validity. The standard deviation is the interval of score differences that indicates levels of achievement. The raw score is the basic score usually obtained by counting the number of answers right. It can also be obtained by using the number of wrong answers. The authors of the test can determine any other way to define a raw score.

29. **A high school counselor is the end-of-course examinations coordinator for her school. While preparing for test administration, she must follow all of the following procedures except:**
    (Easy) (Competency 8.0)

    A. Safeguarding the tests

    B. Informing the students of the nature of the test by giving them questions from the test

    C. Guarding the tests in the exam room when students have access to the room

    D. Guarding the tests by not leaving them where students and non-authorized personnel have access

Answer: B. Informing the students of the nature of the test by giving them questions from the test
Since one of the goals of counseling is to build realistic self-concepts, counselors must provide ways to offer useful feedback. Testing can be one of the tools to help students recognize their resources, utilize their strengths and accept their limitations. If students are provided with the test ahead of time, a true picture of the student's abilities and self-concept is not being identified. There is a distinct difference between counseling and instruction; the counselor's job is not to "teach the test" but to inform students of the objectives and testing parameters prior to the event.

30. **The written report of test results and interpretation should not:**
    (Average Rigor) (Competency 8.0)

    A. Be written in understandable language

    B. Always include charts and graphs

    C. Be disseminated on a need to know basis

    D. Be written in the language of testing

Answer: B. Always include charts and graphs
Visual representations, while sometimes useful, in a report of test results are not necessary for understanding them; thus, it is not a critical element of the report.

31. **A high school counselor is responsible for designing a workshop to help parents interpret test data. In order to ensure accurate test interpretation by others, he must follow all the following guidelines except:**
    (Rigorous) (Competency 8.0)

    A. A uniform method of recording should be employed

    B. Consistency in language used should be employed

    C. The purpose, limitations, and the validity of the test should be stated

    D. The receiver of the results should be required to contact the counselor in order to receive the counselor's candid opinion

Answer: D. The receiver of the results should be required to contact the counselor in order to receive the counselor's candid opinion
While it is not in appropriate to contact the counselor for further explanation or clarification of test results, seeking a "candid opinion" can misconstrue or confound the nature of the results.

32. Joe's parents are concerned about Joe's performance in school and on recent achievement tests. He has been evaluated by an outside agency's psychologist regarding IQ and learning ability who believes he is underperforming. Which of the following would be the BEST next step for the school counselor?
(Rigorous) (Competency 9.0)

   A. Offer to meet with the student and his parents to review all the tests and explore what might be going on

   B. Offer to meet with the outside psychologist to review all the tests and explore what might be going on

   C. Ask the parents to have the outside psychologist send the test results to the school counselor

   D. Refer the parents back to the outside psychologist for further testing

Answer: A. Offer to meet with the student and his parents to review all the tests and explore what might be going on
Although options B, C, and D might be useful at some point, the next step is to meet with the parents and the student to gather more information. Reviewing all the test results together, along with asking the student about his experience in school, will help the counselor work with the student and the parents to identify any problems and determine an action plan.

33. **If tests need to be interpreted in a group, the school counselor should not:**
(Easy) (Competency 9.0)

   A. Announce individual test scores

   B. Explain the norm group to which the students have been compared

   C. Provide for private individual interpretation for students

   D. Explain statistics of the test so students can understand the meaning of their scores

Answer: A. Announce individual test scores
The answers listed in b, c, and d support appropriate sharing of information in a group setting. Providing information about an individual to a group is not only detrimental to the student-counselor relationship, but it is also unethical.

34. **In helping a student plan her course of study, the counselor should review and interpret test results with the student. In doing so, the school counselor should not:**
    (Average Rigor) (Competency 9.0)

    A. Relate the results to the goals that had previously been determined

    B. Provide for individual interpretation

    C. Wait to interpret the tests when the student is scheduling the following year's courses

    D. Give the student input into the interpretation of the test results

Answer: C. Wait to interpret the tests when the student is scheduling the following year's courses
The work of a school counselor is to help the student maximize their performance. If a counselor delays in providing information to a student, it could contribute to student failure instead of success.

35. **When interpreting test results for other professionals and parents, the school counselor is not required to:**
    (Average Rigor) (Competency 9.0)

    A. Be thoroughly familiar with the test

    B. Let other staff members see the results of the test

    C. Notify the student that the counselor will be sharing the results with their parent/guardian(s)

    D. Work with the parents in a counseling relationship to help them understand their child's abilities

Answer: B. Let other staff members see the results of the test
Sharing test results with other staff should first be discussed with the student and the student's parents. Depending on the nature of the test, other personnel often do not need to know the results and it best to keep it confidential. The confidential nature of the counseling role demands caution in the dissemination of information concerning students.

36. **When interpreting testing data from other professionals and testing firms, the counselor should do all the following except:**
(Average Rigor) (Competency 9.0)

   A. Understand the material in the report

   B. Go right to the summary and not worry about the technical aspects of the report

   C. Contact the writer of the report for clarification if needed

   D. Refer to the testing manual for clarification if needed

Answer: B. Go right to the summary and not worry about the technical aspects of the report

It is important that the counselor provide an explanation that honors the purpose and motivation for the testing. Looking at the technical aspects of the report may offer important information to this end.

Use this scenario to answer the next three questions (37-39):

> *Counselor:* When we talked the other day, you shared with me that you overheard your parents discussing a divorce, and I know that was a very, very difficult thing for you to hear. How are you feeling today?
>
> *Student:* I'm really angry at both of them, and I wish they would stop trying to pretend everything is okay.
>
> *Counselor:* You mentioned that you felt more comfortable talking with your mom about the situation than your dad. Have you had an opportunity to talk with her about it?
>
> *Student:* No, not yet. I just don't know what to say to her.
>
> *Counselor:* Why don't we practice that today? Let's try this: Turn your chair to face this empty chair, and pretend that your mom is sitting right here in front of you. How do you feel about trying that?
>
> *Student:* I don't know. It seems kind of weird, but I guess we could try.

37. **The student's response to the counselor's initial question indicates which of the following?**
    (Rigorous) (Competency 10.0)

    A. The student and counselor have established a comfortable rapport with one another

    B. The student does not have an accurate understanding of the situation between his parents

    C. The student is avoiding his own concerns by blaming the situation on his parents

    D. The student's anger at his parents hinders his ability to address school-related issues

Answer: A: The student and counselor have established a comfortable rapport with one another
The ease with which the student shares with the counselor indicates that a previous session has helped to establish rapport between student and counselor. Very few details have been discussed at this point; therefore the other options are not appropriate choices.

38. **The counselor's behavior throughout the session indicates that her objective was to:**
    (Rigorous) (Competency 10.0)

    A. Encourage the student to take responsibility for his part in the problem

    B. Help the student learn to mediate the problems between his parents

    C. Help the student communicate his concerns more effectively

    D. Help the student work through his anger toward his parents

Answer: C: Help the student communicate his concerns more effectively
The counselor's objective is never to learn personal information about a student for alternative purposes. This situation does not indicate that the student has any responsibility in the problem, and the counselor would never encourage a student to attempt to mediate a situation between divorcing parents. While the session may help the student to work through anger, the primary objective is to help the student to communicate more effectively

39. **Suggesting the empty chair technique indicates that the counselor's objective was to do which of the following?** *(Rigorous) (Competency 10.0)*

   A. To give the student a safe environment in which to express his concerns to his mother.

   B. To help the student practice working through his anger toward his mother before the actual confrontation.

   C. To show the student how irrational his behavior has become.

   D. To gain a better understanding of the situation between the student's parents.

Answer: A: To give the student a safe environment in which to express his concerns to his mother. Options C and D are irrelevant. The objective is to give the student an opportunity to express his concerns in a safe environment because he may or may not ever have a follow up conversation with his mother. Answer B is incorrect because the counselor does not wish to encourage the student to engage in a confrontation.

40. **Jason enters the school counselor's office distraught over a recent breakup with his girlfriend of 6 months. He tells the counselor that if he could just make better grades and if he could wear nicer clothes and have more friends, he could win back his girlfriend. The counselor begins by examining Jason's irrational thoughts, which is an example of which of the following theories:**
(Rigorous) (Competency 10.0)

   A. Reality Therapy

   B. Gestalt Therapy

   C. Rational Emotive Behavior Therapy

   D. Behavior Therapy

Answer: C. Rational Emotive Behavior Therapy
The key phrase here is "examining Jason's irrational thoughts." Reality therapy, Gestalt therapy, and behavior therapy involve therapeutic practices that analyze rational versus irrational thoughts. The correction of these irrational thoughts and the identification of the reality of the moment is the basis of rational-emotive therapy.

41. Alexandra is having difficulty relating to her classmates and often uses backstabbing as a mechanism to make friends. In a counseling session, the counselor confronts Alex with a number of details that push her to take responsibility for her own actions. This is an example of:
(Rigorous) (Competency 10.0)

   A. Reality Therapy

   B. Existentialist Therapy

   C. Behavior Therapy

   D. Person-Centered Therapy

Answer: A. Reality Therapy
Confrontation and taking responsibility for one's actions are key steps in Reality Therapy. Reality therapy is highly effective when used in school counseling settings with target-specific problems.

42. A school counselor is conducting small group sessions in which students participate in role-playing exercises to learn more effective communication skills. The small group offers all of the following except:
(Average Rigor) (Competency 11.0)

   A. The presence of a built in support system

   B. A non-threatening atmosphere

   C. The substitution of the group for the real world, permitting clients unlimited time to make adjustments

   D. The counselor can reach more clients

Answer: C. The substitution of the group for the real world, permitting clients unlimited time to make adjustments
The key words to focus on are "substitute" and "unlimited." The group experience is a one that provides individuals within the group to disclose and challenge problems as well as practice new skills. Due a variety of possible constraints, it should never be assumed that the opportunity of counseling is unlimited. Group counseling creates an alternative environment which clients sometimes begin to associate with to the exclusion of other aspects of their lives, further distorting views of reality.

TEACHER CERTIFICATION STUDY GUIDE

43. **A high school counselor is running an aggression replacement small group. Throughout the process, he has noted some positive outcomes of group counseling, as well as a few limitations. These limitations include all of the following except:** *(Rigorous) (Competency 11.0)*

    A. There is pressure to accept group values without analyzing them

    B. Some of the students are changing their behavior much more quickly than the others

    C. One of the students seems to have significant problems with impulse control in spite of the group's feedback

    D. A few individuals in the group are justifying their behavior due to reinforcement from the group

Answer: B. Some of the students are changing their behavior much more quickly than the others

Although group members may change at different rates, this is not generally a limitation. It can actually be useful in modeling behavior change to the other group members. Option C is a limitation of group counseling, in that it may be that the student needs more than the group can offer.

44. A middle school counselor is organizing a support group for students affected by a recent disaster – major flooding that displaced a number of families. Which of the following would be the least important in setting up this group? *(Rigorous) (Competency 11.0)*

   A. Limiting the group to a specific grade level

   B. Limiting the group to no more than 10 students

   C. Seeking parental permission for student participation

   D. Ensuring that the students will be able to make up any school work from classes they miss when attending the group

Answer: A. Limiting the group to a specific grade level
Some groups function most effectively when the students are at the same developmental, age or grade level. In this case, since the focus of the group is an external event, age level is less significant. Some groups also function best when the group is limited to 6-8 students, in order to allow for more interpersonal interchange. In this case, the slightly larger group is likely to function to just as well given the issue at hand, and may be necessary to meet the demand. However, the counselor may need to make a special effort to ensure that all students are given a chance to talk as needed. Options C and D are always necessary considerations in running a group for students in the school setting.

45. A group of students in ninth grade have been fighting with each other. Upon meeting with the students, the counselor learns that many of the fights are precipitated by arguments between two groups of students who come from the two middle schools they previously attended. Which of the following group guidance approaches would be least appropriate in this situation?
(Rigorous) (Competency 12.0)

   A. Teaching core concepts about diversity and tolerance in a large group assembly

   B. Leading anger management sessions in a small group format

   C. Holding a meeting for parents and students to discuss the problem

   D. Training students in peer mediation

Answer: C. Holding a meeting for parents and students to discuss the problem.
Although meeting with the parents as a group may be useful at some point, the other options provide students with skills to change their behavior and are more effective long term approaches. Some contact with the parent/guardians is important for success, and they need to be informed of both the problem (in-group/out-group fighting) and the proposed remedies.

46. As part of the continued response to the situation in the previous question, the school counselor implements a violence prevention program. It utilizes all of the following interventions except:
(Average Rigor) (Competency 12.0)

   A. Conflict resolution seminars

   B. Behavior modification programs

   C. Training faculty and staff to intervene before violent confrontations occur

   D. Instituting a boxing program to train students to protect themselves

Answer: D. Instituting a boxing program to train students to protect themselves
Students can be taught to respect the rights of others by programs of cooperation and conflict resolution. The violence prevention program should not promote, encourage, or prepare students to engage in physical retaliation. A boxing program is outside the scope of violence prevention.

TEACHER CERTIFICATION STUDY GUIDE

47. An elementary school counselor conducts a needs assessment to determine specific issues facing his students and the faculty of his school. In the process, he discovers that there is a need for a new program. The need for this specialized program may be indicated by each of the following factors except:
   (Rigorous) (Competency 12.0)

   A. Increased classroom management problems

   B. Available grant money

   C. The completion of a formal needs assessment

   D. Teacher or counselor observations

Answer: B. Available grant money
Classroom problems, teacher or counselor observations and formal needs assessments are all reasons to consider developing a specialized program. The availability of grant money for a special program should not dictate program development; such efforts only make sense if there is also a demonstrated need for the program.

48. A high school counselor plans to implement a peer-mentoring program. In order to ensure confidentiality, promote effectiveness, and foster a safe environment for all participants, she should:
   (Average Rigor) (Competency 12.0)

   A. Not be present when students are conducting a group

   B. Choose the leaders from potential drop-outs

   C. Try not to let parents know what the process involves, so the students can have privacy

   D. Have the student leaders go through an extensive period of training by a professional

Answer: D. Have the student leaders go through an extensive period of training by a professional
Adequate training is important to the success of any peer leadership program, along with good supervision. Counselor presence, parental notification and good selection of student leaders are all important components of success.

TEACHER CERTIFICATION STUDY GUIDE

49. Data included in the initial referral of a child to a counselor should not include:
    (Easy) (Competency 13.0)

    A. Unverified illegal behavior

    B. Academic history

    C. Behavior and discipline history

    D. Family history

Answer: A. Unverified illegal behavior
This information has no place in an initial referral to a counselor. If through the process of working with the student there are behaviors of concern (especially when the student is in danger to self or someone else), the counselor should communicate them to the appropriate individuals such as parent/guardian(s), social services and possibly a school administrator.

50. Procedures for referring a student to an outside agency do not include this information:
    (Easy) (Competency 13.0)

    A. The counselor believes there may be a need for long-term counseling

    B. The parent feels the child has an emotional problem and asks for an evaluation

    C. The counselor is mandated to report a sexual abuse case

    D. The student doesn't like the counselor

Answer: D. The student doesn't like the counselor
This situation may provide an important learning or growth opportunity for both the student and the counselor if handled in an appropriate, timely and ethical manner. It is not a reason for referral.

TEACHER CERTIFICATION STUDY GUIDE

51. A school counselor creating a parent resource center in his office should make available which of the following resources for his clients: *(Easy) (Competency 13.0)*

    A. Mental health referrals

    B. Food banks and government aid programs

    C. Local support groups

    D. All of the above

Answer: D. All of the above
School counselors are key to providing families with resources about many topics and needs beyond the obvious ones such as financial aid and vocational training.

52. The death of a fourth grader in a sledding accident has prompted the implementation of the school crisis response plan. Which of the following would not be included as an appropriate activity in the plan: *(Easy) (Competency 14.0)*

    A. Getting accurate information out to all members of the school community

    B. Sharing the latest media reports about the accident with staff and students

    C. Offering crisis/grief counseling to all students

    D. Providing information to parents and guardians about common stress and grief reactions

Answer: B. Sharing the latest media reports about the accident with staff and students. Although the media may provide some useful information, for the most part, attending to news reports if not helpful in providing good crisis intervention. Crisis responders need to get information from reliable sources, such as emergency management or law enforcement personnel. Further, the sensationalistic nature of news reports can feed fear and create unnecessary anxiety.

53. A bomb threat is reported at the high school, and the school is evacuated. In order to function appropriately as a crisis responder in this situation, the school counselor needs all of the following except:
(*Average Rigor*) *(Competency 14.0)*

   A. A chance to debrief and get support from colleagues

   B. Clarity about roles and responsibilities

   C. Mandatory post-trauma counseling

   D. Adequate training and follow-up

Answer: C. Mandatory post-trauma counseling.
Most crisis responders, with adequate training and support, will recover from the effects of providing crisis intervention. In some cases, professional counseling may be helpful or necessary. However, mandating such counseling is inappropriate.

54. A school counselor is asked to develop a crisis management plan for her school. She includes all of the following in the plan except:
(*Average Rigor*) *(Competency 14.0)*

   A. Specific lines of communication

   B. The name of the crisis team leader

   C. Goals of the plan

   D. Intervention strategies

Answer: B. The name of the crisis team leader
Although designating a crisis team leader is an important part of a crisis management plan, the team leader's name may change over time or in different situations. Writing the plan so it can be used in varied events will make it most useful and comprehensive.

55. A student enters the school counselor's office and displays signs of child abuse and neglect, which include all of the following except: *(Easy) (Competency 15.0)*

   A. Old clothing

   B. Frequent bone fractures

   C. Self-destructive behavior

   D. Poor hygiene

Answer: A. Old clothing
It would be making assumption about the state of the clothing and the family situation. If there is a concern about a student's welfare, the counselor can follow up using appropriate channels and methods.

56. A seventh grade student reports to her counselor that she is concerned about a friend, whom she believes to be taking prescription medications that she purchases from a classmate. The counselor asks the student to elaborate on the reasons she believes her friend is using and deduces that she is correct based on all of the following indicators except: *(Easy) (Competency 15.0)*

   A. Non-participation in athletic activities

   B. Attention problems

   C. Bizarre behavior

   D. Unawareness of surroundings

Answer: A. Non-participation in athletic activities
Students with substance abuse issues may elect or continue to participate in athletic opportunities. However, if there is a pattern of inconsistent attendance or exhibits of behavior that is not customary for the student (providing that there is not a known medical or physical condition), follow-up is indicated.

TEACHER CERTIFICATION STUDY GUIDE

57. A high school counselor is concerned that a female student has anorexia nervosa. She bases this hunch on all of the following except: *(Easy) (Competency 15.0)*

    A. Malnutrition

    B. Behavior regression

    C. No outward signs but observations of the student not eating lunch

    D. Recognizable weight loss

Answer: C. No outward signs but observations of the student not eating at lunch. There are significant outward signs when a person is struggling with anorexia nervosa. Not eating is not necessarily an indicator of anorexia.

58. A counselor notices an eighth grade student who has begun to wear a jacket every day despite warm temperatures. She also knows the family has been stressed lately with several issues. When the counselor talks with the student, she discovers that the student is self-injuring. The student explains that she is cutting herself because she is:
(Average Rigor) (Competency 15.0)

    A. Suicidal

    B. Overly focused on what others think of her

    C. Trying to get attention

    D. Expressing emotional pain in a physical way

Answer: D. Expressing emotional pain in a physical way
Self-injury is an attempt to convey and release emotional pain and tension through cutting, hitting or other form of self-harm. While students who self-injure may need attention or help, they generally don't self-injure just to get attention nor are they suicidal. They may or may not be concerned with what others think of them.

59. In classroom discussion following a video on civil rights and violence, twelfth grade students express opinions about the effects of stereotyping and prejudice on victims. They determine these effects include all of the following except:
(Rigorous) (Competency 15.0)

    A. The necessity to confront the perpetrator

    B. The development of a sense of inferiority

    C. The development of a persecution complex

    D. Thoughts of violence toward the perpetrator

Answer: A. The necessity to confront the perpetrator
To confront a perpetrator could lead to a potentially dangerous altercation between to the victim and the perpetrator. Although in some structured situations and with sufficient planning this can be a healing event for victim and/or perpetrator, it is not a necessity.

60. Florita has recently enrolled in the high school after moving here from Guatemala. The school counselor has reached out to the parents but has not had much luck in getting a response to her overtures. In an effort to improve the situation, the counselor might do all of the following except:
(Rigorous) (Competency 16.0)

    A. Get more information about Guatemalan culture and beliefs

    B. Talk with Florita about her parents' feelings about being in the U.S.

    C. Ask Florita about her parents' language needs

    D. Contact a counselor she knows who has worked with Latin American students for insight and information

Answer: B. Talk with Florita about her parents' feelings about being in the U.S.
Although this might be important information, it is not appropriate for the counselor to put Florita in the position of disclosing such personal information about her parents. Clarifying the parents' language capacity and needs may be appropriate, as would the other options.

61. A school counselor is confused by his repeated inability to connect with students of races other than his own. He feels that he is respectful and interested in them, but they and their parents/guardians, never seem to really talk with him or accept his suggestions. He attends a workshop on cultural competence and learns all of the following except:
(Rigorous) (Competency 16.0)

A. The best way to become more culturally competent is to attend a series of workshops on the topic

B. He needs to learn more about his students' cultural backgrounds

C. He has made assumptions about what his students feel and think that are probably inaccurate

D. Just being sensitive to differences isn't enough; it's only a first step

Answer: A. The best way to become more culturally competent is to attend a series of workshops on the topic
Although education and training can be helpful in gaining cultural competence, more important is the counselor's willingness to be self-reflective, to learn more about different cultures and beliefs, and to find ways to communicate that reflect cultural sensitivity and awareness.

Use this scenario to answer the next three questions (62-64):

Counselor: You mentioned that you have some concerns about your coursework as far as the colleges to which you are applying. Walk me through your concerns, and we'll address them one at a time.

Student: Well, first of all, I was thinking that I only had to complete three Social Studies credits to graduate, but it looks like all of my college choices require four credits. What am I going to do to make up the fourth credit? I already have my schedule for next year, and I have seven classes already selected.

Counselor: Let's take a look at your schedule and see what we need to do. I see that you're planning to take Art and Choir next year, and from what I remember, you really enjoy fine arts courses.

Student: I really do want to take those fine arts classes. I think I may major in Art Education in college. I don't really want to drop either of those classes.

Counselor: I understand that you want to take both, so you're going to need to make a choice based on your goals and on what's best for you. You can take both art classes next year and possibly go to summer school for a Social Studies credit, or…

Student: No, I definitely don't want to go to summer school!

Counselor: Okay, we could look at colleges that only require three credits, or we could change one fine arts class to a Contemporary Issues or Psychology/Sociology course. If we do that, you would be able to meet your fourth requirement for Social Studies for your colleges. What do you think?

Student: Well, I really, really want to participate in both arts classes, but I think this is more important. I sing in my church choir, and I'm a member of Art Club. I guess I'll just take art and change my choir class to Contemporary Issues. I've heard that's a great class.

Counselor: That's an excellent choice. You'll really enjoy that class. What an easy fix! So, what's next?

62. **The student's response to the counselor's initial suggestion for schedule changes indicates which of the following:**
    (Rigorous) (Competency 17.0)

    A. The student is unwilling to consider the counselor's suggestions at this time.

    B. The student is only interested in having fun.

    C. The student is focusing more on minute details than on choices that directly affect his college plans.

    D. The student sees the arts classes as more important to his future than the Social Studies classes.

    Answer: C. The student is focusing more on minute details than on choices that directly affect his college plans. At this point in the session, the student is looking at details rather than the big picture. He is not interested in only having fun, he is not resistant or unwilling to consider the counselor's suggestions, and he does not believe that the counselor is not looking out for his best interest. Answer D is a good answer, but C is the best option.

63. **The counselor's objective throughout the session is which of the following:**
    (Rigorous) (Competency 17.0)

    A. To influence the student to make choices based on his parents' wishes.

    B. To help the student to take responsibility for his decisions.

    C. To influence the student to make choices based on the counselor's wishes.

    D. To empower the student to make the best decision for himself based on several options.

    Answer: D. To empower the student to make the best decision for himself based on several options. The counselor's job is never to "influence" a student to make decisions based on anyone else's wishes. Also, the student is not having difficulty taking responsibility for his decisions. The counselor wants to give the student the most information possible so that the student can make an informed decision with outcomes in his own best interest.

64. **Which of the following is MOST likely to occur following this session:**
    (Rigorous) (Competency 17.0)

    A. Based on the success of his previous decision, the student will feel confident in making additional choices about his schedule.

    B. The student will feel as though the counselor is patronizing him.

    C. The student will make the rest of his decisions without input from the counselor.

    D. The student will feel obligated to ask for the counselor's help in making scheduling decisions in the future.

Answer: A. Based on the success of his previous decision, the student will feel confident in making additional choices about his schedule.
The counselor helped the student to see the "big picture" while making his decisions for schedule changes. The student made the decisions independently with only encouragement form the counselor, so it is likely that he will feel inclined to consult with the counselor in the future. However, he has been empowered to make decisions on his own, as well.

65. **Similarities in theories of vocational choice are all of the following except:**
    (Average Rigor) (Competency 18.0)

    A. They describe the relationship between two sets of observations

    B. They incorporate a variety of theories

    C. They consider family influence on vocational choice a primary consideration

    D. They are usually based upon personality theory

Answer: C. They consider family influence on vocational choice a primary consideration
The primary influences on vocational choice include personality and level of education. Vocational choice theories place very little emphasis on the influence of family as a major factor. Family influence can have a direct impact on educational achievement but only an indirect, minor impact on vocational choice.

TEACHER CERTIFICATION STUDY GUIDE

66. An eighth grade student reports to her counselor that she will be working with a political campaign to earn volunteer hours for her philanthropy club. Her responsibilities will include designing yard signs and going door to door to meet potential voters. It is likely that she would be categorized under which occupational environments based on Holland's theory:
    (Rigorous) (Competency 18.0)

    A. Artistic and social

    B. Realistic and investigative

    C. Enterprising and investigative

    D. Social and conventional

Answer: A. Artistic and social
Artistic and social occupational environments would best match the personality traits of a person who is interested in creative outlets and in working closely with other people, particularly in a "helping" kind of relationship.

67. A school counselor finds Super's theory of vocations helpful in working with students on exploring career choices. This theory is based upon all of the following except:
    (Average Rigor) (Competency 18.0)

    A. The inheritance of psychic energies

    B. The development of self-concepts

    C. External conditions that dictate the expression of self-concepts vocationally

    D. Developmental behavior theory

Answer: A. The inheritance of psychic energies
Psychic energy is defined as the drive that propels a person's behavior and psychological functioning. This is not part of Super's theory.

GUIDANCE COUNSELOR

68. While presenting a career exploration unit with eleventh grade students, a school counselor arranges for her students to participate in a job shadowing experience. When preparing the students, she says that the experience should include all of the following except:
   (Easy) (Competency 19.0)

   A. Spending an extended period of time with a particular person in a chosen field

   B. Being paid

   C. A learning experience by the student and the business volunteer

   D. Experiencing the daily routine of a particular business

Answer: B. Being paid
A paid experience or internship is provided with the understanding that services are being provided on behalf on an employee. The true shadowing experience should be experiential and have nothing to do with payment.

69. The role of the counselor in assisting students in exploring career and educational options includes all the following except:
   (Average Rigor) (Competency 19.0)

   A. Have material for exploration easily accessible

   B. Support and encourage students in their search for career choices

   C. Help students form realistic decisions

   D. Explain career choice theories to them

Answer: D. Explain career choice theories to them
The counselor can use one or more career theories or orientations in order to provide a framework for the work they do with students. However, merely explaining theories to students is neither an effective use of the counselor's time nor does it provide practical applications by which the students can use to explore careers and related information.

TEACHER CERTIFICATION STUDY GUIDE

70. **The school counselor has determined that a number of eleventh graders are interested in learning how to write a resume. Which of the following is the least appropriate method for teaching these skills?**
    (Rigorous) (Competency 19.0)

    A. Working with the teachers in the English and business education departments on a unit on resume writing skills to be co-taught by the two departments

    B. Planning a large group assembly to teach the latest methods and styles of resumes utilizing a well-developed PowerPoint presentation

    C. Offering a three-session program on resume-writing for every study hall period over the next two months

    D. Offering a two-session program on resume-writing to be conducted in all eleventh grade English or social studies classes

Answer: B. Planning a large group assembly to teach the latest methods and styles of resumes utilizing a well-developed PowerPoint presentation Although some students may learn some tips from a large group assembly presentation, most students will learn these kinds of skills better in a smaller group setting. Methods need to include interactive modalities and practice options, with feedback from the counselor and/or teachers. The goal should be for each student to produce a basic resume at the end of the program.

TEACHER CERTIFICATION STUDY GUIDE

71. The business education teacher has approached the school counselor to help him with teaching job-interviewing skills. Following a lecture and discussion of key skills, which of the following would be the most effective approach?
(Rigorous) (Competency 19.0)

   A. A role play by the counselor and teacher on how to do a good interview

   B. A role play by the counselor and teacher, followed by a discussion of the students' fears and concerns about interviewing for a job

   C. A role play by the counselor and teacher, followed by practice role plays by the student

   D. A role play by the counselor and teacher, followed by a computerized search of jobs in the students' area of interest

Answer: C. A role-play by the counselor and teacher, followed by practice role-plays by the students
Although all of these options may provide valuable information to students about job interviewing, a chance to actually practice an interview is most likely give students the chance to actually develop the skills they need. A discussion of fears and concerns may be particularly useful after or between practice role play sessions. Job searches should be confined to a separate program or activity, so the focus on learning interviewing skills is not lost.

72. Decision making occurs at all the following critical points in career development except:
(Average Rigor) (Competency 20.0)

   A. When a student enters high school

   B. In selecting an entry level job

   C. When selecting education plans

   D. In changing jobs

Answer: A. When a student enters high school
According to Roe and Ginzberg, Ginzberg, Axelrad & Herm, the high school years mark a period of exploration in a person's career development. This process of exploration can provide insight to a possible career choice but is not focused on decision making, per se

GUIDANCE COUNSELOR

73. A high school counselor is creating a career education center in her office, which will include written materials, games, interest inventories, and computers designated for career exploration. She is in the process of evaluating materials to be included in her career center. She looks for all of the following except:
(Average Rigor) (Competency 20.0)

   A. Appropriate vocabulary for the targeted age and reading level

   B. Verified accuracy of the information

   C. Advertisements for career exploration tools

   D. The avoidance of biased and stereotyping images

Answer: C. Advertisements for career exploration tools.
Counselors must use their research skills to discern appropriate career materials. While they may want to look at ads to evaluate actual new materials for future use, including advertising materials in an education center is not appropriate.

74. The career information should include all of the following areas except:
(Average Rigor) (Competency 20.0)

   A. The impressions of the reader as indicated by filling out an evaluation form

   B. The preparation required for entry level jobs

   C. The work setting and conditions of the career

   D. The long-term employment outlook

Answer: A. The impressions of the reader as indicated by filling out an evaluation form
The phrase "impressions of the reader" denotes one of subjectivity instead of specific points that can provide the most comprehensive picture of a respective career. Guidelines for the preparation and evaluation of career and occupational literature have been compiled by the National Career Development Association (NCDA).

75. **An eighth grader is very interested in both science and music. She is thinking about her schedule for ninth grade and is uncertain which choices to consider regarding classes. She visits her school counselor to think this through. Which of the following options would be most appropriate?**
(Rigorous) (Competency 20.0)

- A. The counselor suggests the student take the basic courses in ninth grade science to see how she does before committing herself to any plan of action

- B. The counselor discusses a career interest inventory tool with the student, and offers to meet with the student once it has been completed and scored, so they can discuss the student's options based on more information

- C. The counselor recommends intelligence testing by the school psychologist to determine the student's capacity for science and music

- D. The counselor signs the student up for as two science classes and high school chorus for ninth grade, telling the student that this plan will put her on track for the most options in the future

Answer: B. The counselor discusses a career interest inventory tool with the student, and offers to meet with the student once it has been completed and scored, so they can discuss the student's options based on more information.

The basic question the student is bringing has to do with interest and possible future choices. Gathering more information by using a career interest inventory, among other tools, could be helpful in facilitating the student's choices. Intelligence is not an issue here. The counselor should not simply "sign up" the student for classes since the bigger picture includes career development pathways and enhancing decision-making skills.

76. Post secondary education opportunities are not offered in:
    (*Average Rigor*) *(Competency 21.0)*

    A. Vocational training

    B. Community colleges

    C. The military

    D. Practical experience

Answer: D. Practical experience
Post-secondary education is an organized learning experience in which, at the end of a certain time interval, a degree is awarded to signify the completion or mastery of certain skills. While much can be learned from a practical experience such as internships or shadowing, an individual does not earn a degree or certificate. Options A, B, and C are opportunities that afford an individual to learn a skill set, be awarded a degree, and then apply for professional work experiences.

77. Post-secondary educational opportunities do not depend on:
    (*Average Rigor*) *(Competency 21.0)*

    A. The type of career in which the individual has an interest

    B. The abilities of the individual

    C. The social status of the individual

    D. The costs involved in attending

Answer: C. The social status of the individual
Social status will only be a determining factor if an individual allows it to be.

78. **Reliable sources of information on scholarships and financial aid do not include:** *(Easy) (Competency 21.0)*

   A. The guidance counselor

   B. Local scholarships

   C. Newspaper advertisements and paid financial aid sources

   D. Local and guidance department libraries

Answer: C. Newspaper advertisements and paid financial aid sources
Counselors, parents and students need to be cautious about advertisements for scholarships and financial aid. It is important that such opportunities be thoroughly investigated. If money is asked for up front in order to apply for a scholarship, applicants should not apply. It is likely that such an opportunity is a moneymaking scam. There are a variety of sources that can be used to determine if a source is legitimate.

79. **Financial aid specifically earmarked for women and minorities is least likely to be found in:**
   (Average Rigor) (Competency 21.0)

   A. General financial aid references

   B. Minority and women's organizations

   C. The publication "The Higher Education Money Book for Women and Minorities"

   D. Local minority houses of worship

Answer: A. General financial aid references
Options B, C, and D address the sources that are specific to students seeking scholarships for minorities and women. It is important when seeking scholarships with specific criteria to research sources that provide that particular information.

80. **When conducting a needs assessment, a school counselor should request input from which of the following:**
    (Rigorous) (Competency 22.0)

    A. Students only

    B. Administrators only

    C. People in the community who have no students in school

    D. The community, students, staff, administrators, and parents

Answer: D. The community, students, staff, administrators, and parents
It is imperative that all members of the school community including parents are given the opportunity to provide feedback about guidance counseling services; this is the only way in which counselors will generate a clear picture of the needs of the community. The integration of all stakeholders is key to the success of any needs assessment.

81. **A school counselor evaluating the effectiveness of specific programs should consider all of the following except:**
    (Rigorous) (Competency 22.0)

    A. How well the program fits preconceived ideas of intended outcomes

    B. Statistical significance

    C. Interpretation of the meaning of the results

    D. The practicality of implementing the program into every day use

Answer: A. How well the program fits preconceived ideas of intended outcomes
Evaluative data and the practicality of implementing a program for everyday use should guide the determination of the value of a program. Fitting into preconceived goals is not necessarily useful in assessing a program's worth.

TEACHER CERTIFICATION STUDY GUIDE

82. **Program objectives are:**
    (Average Rigor) (Competency 22.0)

    A. Created to fit the outcomes of the research

    B. Readjusted as the need arises

    C. Determined after the program has been operational for a period of time

    D. Formulated before the research is instituted

Answer: D. Formulated before the research is instituted

An effective guidance program needs to be based on research in order to be sound in its validity. Objectives need to be clearly established prior to any research or assessment efforts.

83. **In his first year at a new elementary school, a school counselor is excited to implement a number of new programs with his students. In order to implement the most effective programs, the counselor should begin by doing which of the following:**
    (Rigorous) (Competency 22.0)

    A. Ask the administration for a budget for the program

    B. Conduct a needs assessment survey

    C. Arrange for a pilot program

    D. Contact Board of Education members to get them to agree on the implementation of the program

Answer: B. Conduct a needs assessment survey
Just because a program is innovative and has a lot to offer does not mean it will meet the needs of the respective school community. It is critical for school counselors to have a pulse on the needs of the community they serve. It is imperative that the school counselor develops a program improvement model that clearly outlines action steps for the creation, monitoring, and support of any and all programs that are utilized.

84. Choose the best answer in evaluating the following statement: (Rigorous) (Competency 23.0)

Counselor: (to a teacher) "Do you mind if I ask you about Shandra? She came to me with something personal and I'm not sure what to do. Can we talk?"

    A. Appropriate, because the teacher knows Shandra and her family quite well and may provide some insight.

    B. Appropriate, because the counselor needs to get a second opinion.

    C. Inappropriate, because counselors need to respect students' privacy and not discuss personal matters with teachers. An appropriate consult would be with another counselor.

    D. Inappropriate, because the teacher knows the student personally.

Answer: C. Inappropriate, because counselors need to respect students' privacy and not discuss personal matters with teachers. An appropriate consult would be with another counselor.

Keeping confidences in a school community can be difficult when many teachers and students know each other outside the school setting. Counselors have a duty to be careful to maintain appropriate boundaries. Option D is partially correct, but even if the student was unknown to the teacher, the counselor should seek a consult with another counselor, not a teacher.

85. Choose the best answer in evaluating the counselor's statements in the following scenario:
    (Rigorous) (Competency 23.0)

Student: "Is it okay to talk with you about something private? I mean, do you have to tell someone else anything I tell you? This is really important."

Counselor: "I'm glad you came to me. I keep private everything students tell me, unless you are in danger of hurting yourself or someone else. Then I have to tell someone – that's the law. But let's see what's going on. I really would like to help you."

Student: "But you might have to tell someone. Maybe I shouldn't talk to you."

Counselor: "I will do my best to keep this between us. And I will tell you first if I need to go to someone else, including your parents. In fact, if I call your parents, I would like you to be in the room with me. How's that? We will only go to someone else if we have to. I really want to help."

- A. Appropriate, because she tells the student that she really wants to help her no matter what

- B. Appropriate, because the counselor is both reassuring about the importance of privacy and also honest about the need to disclosure certain information to parents and others

- C. Inappropriate, because the counselor creates anxiety by mentioning the law and possible disclosure

- D. Inappropriate, because the student will feel betrayed by the possible need to disclose the information

Answer: B. Appropriate, because the counselor is both reassuring about the importance of privacy and also honest about the need to disclosure certain information to parents and others.

Counselors need to balance their efforts to invite students to talk with them with their legal and ethical responsibilities. To not tell the student early on that the counselor must disclose certain information will ultimately lead to a greater sense of betrayal for the student. To be up front about this issue AND inviting at the same time can actually build trust.

TEACHER CERTIFICATION STUDY GUIDE

86. In implementing the Michigan Comprehensive Guidance and Counseling Program, a school district does not need to:
(Average Rigor) (Competency 24.0)

   A. Write a specific mission statement consistent with the school district's mission statement and purpose

   B. Provide all four components of the program (guidance curriculum, individual planning, responsive services and systems support) to all grade levels as long as adequate and developmentally appropriate guidance services are provided at each grade level

   C. Do a needs assessment and conduct periodic evaluations of the program for ongoing improvement

   D. Do a needs assessment and have an action plan for implementation

Answer: B. Provide all four components of the program (guidance curriculum, individual planning, responsive services and systems support) to all grade levels as long as adequate and developmentally appropriate guidance services are provided at each grade level
All four components of the program must be present at all grade levels, K-12. The services need to be developmentally appropriate and consistent with the overall program, mission, and purpose.

87. An elementary school counselor is involved with helping families new to the district become acquainted with local resources for their children. This work falls under which component of the Michigan Comprehensive Guidance and Counseling Program:
(Average Rigor) (Competency 24.0)

   A. Guidance Curriculum

   B. Individual Planning

   C. Responsive Services

   D. Systems Support

Answer: C. Responsive Services
Responsive Services includes providing parent/guardian(s) and students with referrals to community resources, facilitating their ability to access those services, and providing appropriate follow-up as needed.

GUIDANCE COUNSELOR

TEACHER CERTIFICATION STUDY GUIDE

88. Which of the following activities fall outside the scope of the Guidance Curriculum as outlined in the Michigan Comprehensive Guidance and Counseling Program:
(Rigorous) (Competency 24.0)

   A. Career Day, psycho-educational group on emotional intelligence, and classes on study skills

   B. Study skills support group, peer counseling program, and on-site college visits

   C. Socio-cultural sensitivity training, computerized career information searches, and mock job interviews

   D. School-to-work programs, personal counseling, and assemblies on violence prevention

Answer: D. School-to-work programs, personal counseling, and assemblies on violence prevention
Personal counseling is not part of the Guidance Curriculum (although school-to-work programs and violence prevention are). Personal counseling falls under a different component of the Comprehensive Program, that of Responsive Services. The three content areas of the Guidance Curriculum are Career Knowledge and Exploration, Knowledge of Self and Others, and Educational/Career-Technical Development.

89. The counseling department of a school district conducts a one day professional development session for all of the counselors in the entire district. Following this initial meeting, the district determines that this event should be repeated on an annual basis, at minimum. Counselors report all of the following positive results except:
(Easy) (Competency 25.0)

   A. They are kept abreast of changes in professional practices and standards

   B. They are able to utilize all available monies in the budget for staff development

   C. They are able to be refreshed and renewed as professionals

   D. They are able to further develop counseling skills

Answer: B. They are able to utilize all available monies in the budget for staff development
Continuing education and development is geared to support and expand the school counselor's capacity to function well. In many cases, the counselor may spend his or her own money to get appropriate training or learn new skills.

GUIDANCE COUNSELOR

TEACHER CERTIFICATION STUDY GUIDE

Use this scenario as a backdrop to answer the next five questions (90-94):
A first-year school counselor realizes early in the school year that she must learn to work closely with the administration, faculty, staff and parents of her students in order to most effectively serve her young students. She begins by administering a needs assessment to all stakeholders and then shares the carefully researched results in a faculty meeting. She requests permission from teachers of various subjects and grade levels to observe classes. When a teacher requests her assistance in working with specific students, she involves that teacher in the process by asking for his or her observations before, during, and after the observation. She also asks for help from her colleagues at other schools for prevention and intervention ideas, as well as ways to promote the school counseling program for the benefit of everyone involved. Before long, she notices that her counselor log is full of appointments, her interventions are becoming more successful, and she can no longer walk down the hall without receiving multiple greetings and questions from teachers, students, and parents.

90. **Procedures in the consultation process include all except:**
    (Average Rigor) (Competency 25.0)

    A. Relationship building

    B. Monitoring of the process of behavior change by a neutral party

    C. Evaluation and summarization

    D. Diagnosis of the problem

Answer: B. Monitoring of the process of behavior change by a neutral party
Consultation is an active, dynamic process. Monitoring is not part of the consultation model.

91. **The role the counselor can take in assisting participants in the consultation process does not include:**
    (Rigorous) (Competency 25.0)

    A. Demonstrating classroom behavior management techniques

    B. Describing the nature of the problem

    C. Teaching specific skills

    D. Helping devise strategies to change behaviors

Answer: A Demonstration of classroom behavior management techniques
The role of the counselor is to observe and provide constructive feedback or to provide direct support in identified areas of need. Classroom behavior management is the educator's responsibility and areas of weakness should be addressed by the school administration. The counselor in this situation is present to offer insight to support individual students from a behavioral and social aspect, not to support the classroom educator and his/her class management

92. **In the consultation process, communicating student's needs to others does not include:**
    (Average Rigor) (Competency 25.0)

    A. Making a judgment by the counselor to others as to what is best for the student

    B. Clarifying the needs of the student with the student

    C. Opening lines of communication between the consultee and the student by having open dialogue

    D. Balancing the needs of the student and the consultee so each can understand the other's position

Answer: A. Making a judgment by the counselor to others as to what is best for the student
Instead of passing judgment, the counselor's role is assist stakeholders in the student's success. The counselor's job is to educate them about the needs of the student based on information gathered from parents and teachers, review the student's academic history, and work with all parties to develop a plan of action

93. **In conducting a consultation follow-up, the counselor should not:**
    (Rigorous) (Competency 25.0)

    A. Gradually decrease participation in the process

    B. Reevaluate after a period of time

    C. Interview the consultee to determine if there is continuing progress

    D. Interview the student and parents in regards to their satisfaction with the consultation

Answer: A. Gradually decrease participation in the process
Follow-up should be ongoing on behalf of the counselor to reevaluate goals and the treatment plan and make adjustments where and when appropriate.

94. **In evaluating the results of consultation, all the following factors should be considered except:**
    (Rigorous) (Competency 25.0)

    A. The feelings of the student's parents as to the success of the process

    B. The report of the consultee as to the problem solving results

    C. An attitude change in the student

    D. Empirical results of an evaluation tool

Answer: D. Empirical results of an evaluation tool
This would serve no effective purpose on the process of consultation. Assessment and monitoring of the evaluation tool is an important step in the process of improving the counseling program, but consideration of the tool should not be considered as a part of each consultation

95. A good orientation program should include each of the following except:
    (Easy) (Competency 26.0)

    A. Advance notice by mail

    B. A tour of the facilities

    C. Invitations to the entire community

    D. Introduction of counselors and administrators to students and parents with a description of their roles

Answer: C. Invitations to the entire community
Part of advocating for the guidance program and its services is to utilize a variety of methods to both inform and invite. This program is designed to inform and invite parents and guardians to engage with the school counselors; it is not a generic public relations open house.

96. When a tenth grade student receives several disciplinary referrals in a short time period, her counselor contacts her parents in order to explain the situation and brainstorm solutions. Throughout the process, the counselor should do all of the following except:
    (Rigorous) (Competency 26.0)

    A. Inform the parents frequently as to the progress of the resolution of the problem

    B. Use parents as a valuable source of information about the student

    C. Accept parents' ideas for behavior modification

    D. Explain the problem in simple language as parents are probably unaware of all ramifications

Answer: D. Explain the problem in simple language, as parents are probably unaware of all ramifications
It is appropriate for the counselor to take into the parent's primary language and understanding of certain procedure. This can be established by fact finding and consulting with the student before contacting the parent/guardian(s). However, it is inappropriate to make assumptions about parents' abilities and the level of understanding they bring to any process.

TEACHER CERTIFICATION STUDY GUIDE

97. **A middle school counselor collaborating with parents in the counseling process for their seventh grade student should expect that the parents will contribute which of the following:** *(Easy) (Competency 26.0)*

   A. Solutions to the presenting problem

   B. Family and medical history, a willingness to participate and possible solutions

   C. Very little, since most parents are uncooperative

   D. Monitoring the child at home

Answer: B. Family and medical history, a willingness to participate and possible solutions.
Regardless of the nature of the information parents provide, inviting the parent to be one of the experts can lead to greater levels of understanding the student's background, strengths, challenges and growth areas. At times, parents' information and suggestions can help create the best possible action plan. Although monitoring the child at home is one of the ways parents and guardians participate, D is not the best or most comprehensive option.

98. **In working with parents, a good model to utilize is:** *(Easy) (Competency 26.0)*

   A. Collaborative consultation

   B. Mental health consultation

   C. Family counseling

   D. Advising

Answer: A. Collaborative consultation
Working with parents and guardians in a collaborative manner where each person is bringing relevant and important information to the table is useful. In a school setting, the counselor should not serve as a mental health consultant or family counselor or advisor.

TEACHER CERTIFICATION STUDY GUIDE

99. **The rights of parents, students, and guardians do not include:**
 (Average Rigor) (Competency 27.0)

   A. Right of access

   B. Right of privacy

   C. Right to challenge and a hearing

   D. Right to alter the written record if they feel it is not true

Answer: D. Right to alter the written record if they feel it is not true
Parents may advocate for personal information to be corrected when they have the appropriate documentation to support the change. However, parents may not request the student's academic record be altered in any way.

100. **Written permission must be obtained to release assessment data from:**
 (Average Rigor) (Competency 27.0)

   A. The counselor

   B. The student over 18 or the student's parent or guardian

   C. The Board of Education

   D. The teacher who generated the assessment data

Answer: B. The student over 18 or the student's parent or guardian
Since counseling is a confidential relationship, the counselor should obtain permission from the student to release any information given in confidence. However, if the student is under 18, even if the information is gathered in reference to services provided due to a disability (i.e. IDEA qualifications), written permission needs to be procured from the parent or legal guardian.

XAMonline, INC. 21 Orient Ave. Melrose, MA 02176
Toll Free number 800-509-4128
TO ORDER Fax 781-662-9268 OR www.XAMonline.com

MICHIGAN TEST FOR TEACHER EXAMINATION - MTTC - 2007

PO# Store/School:
Address 1:

Address 2 (Ship to other):

City, State Zip

Credit card number ___-___-___-___   expiration_____
EMAIL _____
PHONE   FAX

ISBN	TITLE	Qty	Retail	Total
978-1-58197-968-8	MTTC Basic Skills 96		$27.95	
978-1-58197-954-1	MTTC Biology 17		$59.95	
978-1-58197-955-8	MTTC Chemistry 18		$59.95	
978-1-58197-974-9	MTTC Early Childhood Education 82		$73.50	
978-1-58197-966-4	MTTC Elementary Education 83		$28.95	
978-1-58197-950-3	MTTC English 02		$59.95	
978-1-58197-959-6	MTTC French 23		$15.00	
978-1-58197-965-7	MTTC Guidance Counselor 51		$59.95	
978-1-58197-972-5	MTTC Integrated Science 94		$59.95	
978-1-58197-963-3	MTTC Library Media 48		$59.95	
978-1-58197-958-9	MTTC Mathematics 22		$59.95	
978-1-58197-962-6	MTTC Physical Education 44		$59.95	
978-1-58197-871-1	MTTC Physics 19		$59.95	
978-1-58197-952-7	MTTC Political Science 10		$34.95	
978-1-58197-951-0	MTTC Reading 05		$59.95	
978-1-58197-960-2	MTTC Spanish 28		$59.95	
978-1-58197-9732	MTTC Special Education- Emotionally Impaired 59		$59.95	
978-1-58197-953-4	MTTC Learning Disabled 63		$59.95	
978-1-58197-970-1	MTTC Social Studies 84		$59.95	
			SUBTOTAL	
			Ship	$8.25
			TOTAL	

www.ingramcontent.com/pod-product-compliance
Lightning Source LLC
Chambersburg PA
CBHW080537300426
44111CB00017B/2762